The Write Way

A foundation in academic writing for
the humanities, business, and social sciences

A foundation in academic writing for
the humanities, business, and social sciences

THE
WRITE WAY

University College
Sungkyunkwan University

Sungkyunkwan University Press

Contents

The Writing Process

Styles of Writing

Building Blocks

Research Skills

The Writing Process

This section helps students develop and master three basic structures for scientific writing: sentences, paragraphs, essays, and reports. The first part covers different kinds of sentence structure so learners can use a variety of sentence types in their writing. The next part explores paragraphs by explaining how to brainstorm, develop parts of the paragraph, and maintain consistency throughout the entire piece of writing. After learning about paragraphs, students will transition into writing essays including brainstorming, developing introductory paragraphs, structuring body paragraphs, and making effective concluding paragraphs. Finally, students will develop business or social science reports, including introductions, methodology, results, and conclusions. They will cite supporting evidence, and make effective deductions. After completing this section, learners should be more competent and confident in writing well-developed essays and clearly-written reports.

This section covers:

- Format
- Pre-Writing
- Sentences
- Paragraphs
- Essays

1 Format

Unless you are specifically told otherwise, you are expected to type and print writing assignments. It is important that the assignment is arranged and presented in an appropriate way, and this is called "format." The format that is presented here is called Modern Language Association style (MLA). Other styles are available.

Activity 1

The following paragraphs are about the history of Sungkyunkwan University. The content is the same, but the format is different. Read the two paragraphs and pay attention to the format. Identify the errors in the first that are corrected in the second.

Sungkyunkwan University (SKKU) was founded in 1398 as a Confucian school of learning for the privileged and upper class.
The original campus is located in what is now Myeongnyun-dong, Seoul. During the Japanese occupation from 1911, the school was renamed Kyonghagwon, and remained so until 1946 when the occupation ended and the original name, Sungkyunkwan, was restored. Over the next three decades, SKKU grew in size and reputation.
Facing an increasing student enrollment, and restricted by limited space around the campus in central Seoul, SKKU expanded its campus in 1978 and developed a second site in suwon that would house the school of natural sciences.
Currently, the suwon campus has an enrollment of around 15,000 students, up from 5000 when it opened.
Together the two campuses provide the largest center of learning in South Korea, with the greatest student population.

Sungkyunkwan University

Sungkyunkwan University (SKKU) was founded in 1398 as a Confucian school of learning for the privileged and upper class. The original campus is located in what is now Myeongnyun-dong, Seoul. During the Japanese occupation from 1911, the school was renamed Kyonghagwon, and remained so until 1946 when the occupation ended and the original name, Sungkyunkwan, was restored. Over the next three decades, SKKU grew in size and reputation. Facing an increasing student enrollment and restricted by limited space around the campus in central Seoul, SKKU expanded its campus in 1978 and developed a second site in Suwon that now houses the school of natural sciences. Currently, the Suwon campus has an enrollment of around 15,000 students, up from 5,000 when it opened. Together the two campuses provide the largest center of learning in South Korea, with the greatest student population.

» Format Guideline

Line space
Set the line space to 2.0.

Title
All writing assignments require a title centered at the top of the first page.
The title should not be a sentence, and it should follow all of the capitalization,
font, and size guidelines.

Indent
Indent the first line of the paragraph with the TAB key. (Set indent to 1.27cm.)

Size
Use font size 12.

Font
Use a plain font such as Times New Roman. Do not use a fancy font.

Margins
Set margins to 2.54cm in your word processor.

Check
Check your paper for spelling and grammar. Do not make handwritten corrections.

Personal details
Put your full name, class, and student number in the top corner of the first page.

2

Pre-writing

The aim of pre-writing is to focus thoughts, develop ideas, and explore your topic in preparation for writing. There are a number of methods that can be used in pre-writing.

Free Writing

The aim is to write continuously on the page without stopping to think. Write whatever comes to mind, and do not worry about grammar, spelling, or word choice. It can be done on the computer or on paper. You might start with a general topic (for example, jobs) or a theme (for example, descriptive writing), but you can also write completely freely and see what develops.

The keys to effective free writing:
• Set a time limit
• Write for the whole of the allotted time
• Write down everything that comes into your head, regardless of logic or quality

Activity 1

Practice free writing for ten minutes, and then read your work. Were the ideas connected, or did they jump around from topic to topic? Read your partner's work.

List

Listing is a form of brainstorming in which writers list of all the ideas that come to their mind in a set time.

Seoul	Blue House	Hongdae	Crowded
	Cheonggyecheon	Museums	Big
	Universities	City Hall	Pollution
	Subway	Palaces	Exciting
	Capital city	Bus	Han River

Activity 2

In your notebook, list ideas for one of the following topics.

| University | Friend | Sport | Hero |

Mind Map

A mind map is a great way to organize ideas according to relationships or common features.

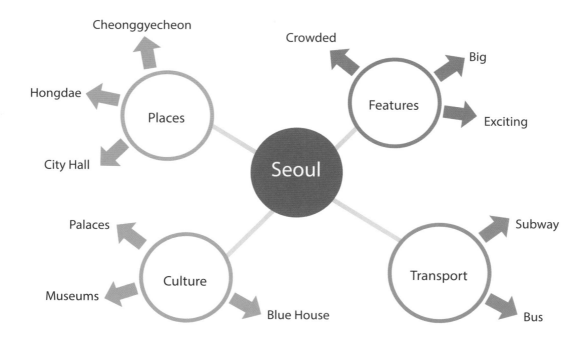

Activity 3

Make a mind map to connect your ideas from Activity 2.

Web Search

These days, the first place people go for ideas is often the Internet. The Internet gives us access to an almost unlimited amount of information, all at our fingertips. While the Internet should not be the only resource, it is a valuable tool.

Activity 4

Use the Internet to research one of the following topics. Use at least three sources.

| Christmas | Chuseok | Easter | Halloween |

Cut and paste the information relevant to the topic into a Word document. Copy the URL for each source onto the document. Each source and its content should be color coded or in a different font. Arrange the information in a logical way so it flows as a single piece. Add a title and list the URLs at the end of the document.

Journal

Many writers keep a journal of thoughts, ideas, and questions. This can be a creative tool for developing ideas for future writing projects.

Activity 5

The methods described in this chapter can be used individually or they can be used together as a longer process. Practice prewriting by following this process.

1. Free write for ten minutes.

2. Take one idea from the free writing section as a topic, and make a list of related ideas.

3. Organize these ideas into a clear, logical mind map.

4. Do a web search on the topic being developed, and gather three good sources.

5. Arrange your ideas and the information from the web search into a logical order.

Sentences

A sentence is a complete idea, and it contains a subject and a verb. In other words, a sentence is composed of one or more clauses, which are grammatical units containing at least an explicit or implied subject, and a predicate. Clauses may be independent (IC) or dependent (DC).

What is an Independent Clause?

An independent clause is the part of a sentence that can stand by itself because it includes a subject, verb, and complete idea.

What is a Dependent Clause?

A dependent clause requires an independent clause to make a complete sentence because it is incomplete by itself.

Types of Sentences

Type of Sentence	Sentence Construction
Simple Sentence	One IC
Compound Sentence	More than one IC, no DC
Complex Sentence	One IC, at least one DC
Compound-Complex Sentence	More than one IC, one or more DC

💡 Grammar Tip

Complete Sentences

- Start with a capital letter.
- Finish with a period (.), a question mark (?), or an exclamation mark (!).
- Contain at least one independent clause (IC), which includes a subject (S), a verb (V), and a complete idea.

Capital letter   S   V   V   Period

A sneaky burglar broke into my house and ate all my spaghetti.

IC

Capital letter   S   V

London's famous underground "Tube" system is in trouble because the ancient infrastructure was not designed to cope with the demands of modern society.

Period

» Sentence Structure and Variety

Because writers do not want to repeatedly use the same type of sentence structure in their writing, they use different types of sentences to make their writing more effective. This section will help students identify and construct different sentence types.

Simple Sentences and Sentence Fragments

The simple sentence is a single clause that includes a subject, verb, and a complete idea. Simple sentences are also known as independent clauses when they are part of longer sentences. Sentences that are incomplete are called sentence fragments.

Examples:

Simple Sentence: The animal was sick.

Sentence Fragment: Because the animal was sick.

Activity 1

Read the following sentences, and identify the subject and verb in each section. If the sentence is a sentence fragment, finish the sentence yourself.

1. The monkeys were hungry.

2. The massive storm destroyed many of the trees in the jungle.

3. While walking in the jungle.

4. Who gave a lecture on gorillas?

5. Who gave a lecture on gorillas.

6. Because the zoo was closed.

7. The biologist gave the school children a tour of the zoo.

8. The biologist who studies monkeys.

9. The conservation program focuses on preserving natural habitat.

10. After the lecture on preserving natural habitat.

Compound Sentences

Compound sentences are two simple sentences joined by a comma with a coordinating conjunction (FANBOYS). Each coordinating conjunction shows a relationship.

Coordinating Conjunctions	Example
For (cause)	He was late for class, **for** he missed the bus.
And (addition)	She is rich, **and** he likes shopping.
Nor (negative choice)	She did not want help, **nor** did she ask for it.
But (contrast)	She wanted to meet her friends, **but** she had to study.
Or (positive choice)	We can go to Caribbean Bay, **or** we can go to Everland.
Yet (contrast/concession)	He is a heavy smoker, **yet** he is a good athlete.
So (effect)	It rained last weekend, **so** the picnic was canceled.

💡 Punctuation Tip

Commas in Compound Sentences

When joining two independent clauses with a conjunction, a comma (,) is used after the first clause and before the conjunction.

Two simple sentences: Rabbits are plant eaters. Tigers eat meat.
One compound sentence: Rabbits are plant eaters, **but** tigers eat meat.

If the sentence contains only one independent clause and a conjunction, a comma is not used because it is not a compound sentence.

Compound sentence: Rabbits eat grass, **and** rabbits eat weeds.
Simple sentence: Rabbits eat grass and weeds.

Activity 2

Write a "C" (compound) or "NC" (not compound) beside the following sentences.

1. Elephants eat leaves and fruit.
2. Elephants eat leaves, fruit, and grass.
3. Elephants eat leaves, fruit, and grass, but they never eat fish.
4. Bats eat so many different kinds of food.
5. Bears sleep most of the winter, so they are hibernating animals.
6. Bats are active at night, for they are nocturnal animals.
7. Camels have one or two humps on their backs.
8. Neither cats nor dogs live in water.
9. Pandas' bodies are suited for eating meat, yet they eat bamboo.
10. Dolphins cannot live on land, nor can whales live on land.

Complex Sentences

Complex sentences are independent clauses joined by subordinating conjunctions to subordinating (or dependent) clauses. In complex sentences, commas are only used if the dependent clause comes first.

Because their tusks are ivory, elephants are sometimes killed by poachers.
Elephants are sometimes killed by poachers **because** their tusks are ivory.

Subordinating Conjunctions

The following table shows the subordinating conjunctions using "ON A WHITE BUS."

Subordinating Words	Example
Only if	I will cook **only if** you wash the dishes.
Now that	**Now that** I feel better, I can go back to work.
After, although, as	**Although** the fish smelled bad, it tasted good.
When, whenever, where, wherever, while, whereas, whether or not	Julia wore glasses **when** she was young.
If, in case	**If** you leave the room, please lock the door.
Though	**Though** she was angry, she smiled.
Even though, even if	**Even** if you are on a diet, you need to eat.
Because, before	**Before** she became a vegetarian, she loved beef.
Unless, until	**Unless** they hurry up, they will be late.
Since, so that	**Since** he was young, he has loved dogs.

Activity 3

Insert an appropriate subordinating conjunction in the following sentences. In addition, identify the independent and dependent clauses.

1. _____ rats carry diseases, people do not want them in homes.

2. _____ baby birds can fly, their parents bring them food.

3. _____ kangaroos are babies, they live in their mother's pouch.

4. _____ many snakes are harmless, many people are afraid of them.

5. Baby frogs can live on land _____ they grow legs and lungs.

6. Sharks do not attack humans _____ they are hungry.

7. _____ skunks feel in danger, they expel a horrible spray.

8. Kittens cannot open their eyes _____ they are born.

Activity 4

Interview your partner. Take notes of your partner's information in your notebook, and use them to write a mix of compound and complex sentences underneath your notes. Use the following questions as a starting point, but make sure you think of some interesting questions of your own.

1. What musical instrument would you like to learn?

2. Which film star would you like to play you in the movie of your life?

3. What do you look for in a boyfriend or girlfriend?

4. What animal best represents you?

5. Which species of animal would you exterminate?

6. Which household chore is your least favorite?

7. Which country would you never want to visit?

8. Which celebrity would you like to meet?

💡 Punctuation Tip

Joining Independent Clauses with Semicolons and Colons

A semicolon (;) can join two related independent clauses.

Example: Mosquitoes can carry malaria; they are also a dengue fever vector.
The second clause may begin with a transition word followed by a comma.

Example: Mosquitoes are usually harmless; however, they can transmit serious diseases such as malaria and dengue fever.

Independent clauses can also be joined by a colon (:) if the second clause is a deduction from the first, or an explanation or illustration of the first.

Example: The patient was diagnosed with malaria after returning from Madagascar: she probably contracted it while there.

Note that colons after independent clauses have another (unrelated) function: they are also used to introduce lists.

Example: Mosquitoes are vectors for several well-known diseases: malaria, dengue fever, yellow fever, Japanese encephalitis, and Zika fever.

Semicolon Practice

Correct the following sentences by using semicolons.

Example: Mosquitoes carry diseases like malaria; they also transmit dengue fever.

Activity 5

Based on the previous punctuation tip, use semicolons to connect the following sentences.

1. Alligators have sharp teeth. They do not make good pets.

_____

2. Cows are raised for their meat. They are also raised for milk.

_____

3. Chickens have wings. They are not able to fly for long periods.

_____

4. Camels store water in their humps. They can walk long distances without water.

_____

Activity 6

Coordinating conjunctions, subordinating conjunctions, and transition word often convey similar relationships. Using the words given, complete the table.

Coordinating conjunctions: for, and, but, yet, so.

Subordinating conjunctions: while, so that, even though, though, since, due to, because, although

Transitions: nevertheless, because of this, on the other hand, therefore, thus.

Relationship	Words
Addition	
Contrast	
Effect	
Cause	

Activity 7

Rewrite the following sentences in another type of sentence. For instance, try changing a compound sentence into a complex sentence.

Example: Mosquitoes are usually harmless; **however**, they sometimes carry diseases. (;)
Mosquitoes are usually harmless, but they sometimes carry diseases. (compound)
Although mosquitoes are usually harmless, they sometimes carry diseases. (complex)

1. Elephants eat leaves, fruit, and grass, but they never eat fish.

_____

2. Because some rats carry diseases, people do not want them in homes.

_____

3. Bears sleep most of the winter, so they are hibernating animals.

_____

4. Pandas' bodies are suited for eating meat, yet they eat bamboo.

_____

5. Although many snakes are harmless, many people are still afraid of them.

_____

6. Elephants eat leaves and fruit, and they also eat grass.

_____

Compound-Complex

This sentence type combines compound and complex sentences, and/or semicolons into the same sentence. The following simple sentences can be combined into one compound–complex sentence.

Original Passage:
The American Kennel Club recognizes over one hundred and fifty dog breeds. Border Collies are one of the most intelligent breeds. Afghan Hounds are considered one of the least intelligent.

Compound-complex Sentence:
The American Kennel Club recognizes over one hundred and fifty dog breeds, **and** Border Collies are one of the most intelligent dog breeds **while** Afghan Hounds are considered one of the least intelligent.

Activity 8

Use the skills practiced so far to combine the following sentences. Remember to use a variety of sentence types.

1. Pigs are often considered dirty. Pigs do not sweat very much. Pigs cover themselves in mud on hot days to keep cool.

_____

_____

2. Rabbits can have four to twelve babies in each pregnancy. Rabbits are pregnant for thirty days. One rabbit can have eight hundred descendants in nine months.

_____

_____

3. Chameleons have many talents. Chameleons can sleep upside down. Chameleons can change color in reaction to temperature changes. Chameleons' eyes can turn independently of one another.

_____

_____

4. Chimpanzees use tools like sticks to find food. Chimpanzees are very similar to humans. The two species share 98.4% of the same genetic material. Chimpanzees can recognize themselves in a mirror.

_____

_____

5. Many oysters change their sex several times in their lives. Shrimp are born male. Shrimp become female as they get older. Some animals do not have a stable sex.

_____

_____

Comma Splices

Comma splices are incomplete sentences that incorrectly combine independent clauses with a comma.

Example:
Horses can sleep standing up, they can also sleep lying down.

There are four ways to correct comma splices:

1. Use a period after the first independent clause to create two separate sentences.
   Horses can sleep standing up. They can also sleep lying down.

2. Insert a semicolon after the first independent clause to create a compound sentence.
   Horses can sleep standing up; they can also sleep lying down.

3. Insert a coordinating conjunction after the comma to create a compound sentence.
   Horses can sleep standing up, and they can also sleep lying down.

4. Insert a subordinating conjunction at the beginning of the clause to create a complex sentence.
   While horses can sleep standing up, they can also sleep lying down.

Activity 9

Correct the following comma splices.

1. Chickens eat seeds, they also eat small animals like lizards or mice.

_____

2. Sheep are raised for their wool, they are also raised for their milk and meat.

_____

3. Many parrots can learn to speak human languages, they are popular as pets.

_____

4. In some areas, tigers are nearly extinct, they are hunted for their beautiful fur.

_____

5. Turtles appeared about 215 million years ago, they are one of the oldest orders of reptiles.

_____

4 Paragraphs

A paragraph is an organizational unit or chunk in writing that comprises a group of sentences on a single theme or topic. Most writing is organized into themed chunks ranging in length from a single sentence to a dozen or more sentences. Regardless of the length, these chunks should develop the main idea in a clear and logical way.

A paragraph may stand by itself or be one part of a longer piece of work. In academic writing, paragraphs are often used to answer short questions, give definitions or descriptions, or give opinions. If you can write good paragraphs, you can write good essays. This unit starts with the essentials of paragraph writing and then moves on to how to combine and expand individual paragraphs to build essays.

Paragraph Structure

A good paragraph usually has three basic parts, as shown in the basic outline below.

Title

1. Topic sentence

2. Supporting sentences
    a. Supporting detail
    b. Supporting detail
    c. Supporting detail

3. Concluding sentence

Title: Africa's Most Dangerous Animal

1. Topic sentence
Africa's most dangerous animal is the hippopotamus.

2. Supporting sentences
a. Physical characteristics – powerful animal, three meters in length, can weigh over three tonnes, can outrun a human, has powerful jaws that can easily bite a person in half.

b. Temperament – very bad tempered, anyone who gets in between an adult hippopotamus and its calf or the water is likely to be attacked.

c. Statistics – Kills more than 500 people each year, more than any other large African animal.

3. Concluding sentence
The power, temperament, and number of victims of the hippopotamus make it the most feared animal in Africa.

When put together, the pieces create a strong outline for a logical and coherent paragraph.

Africa's Most Dangerous Animal

Africa's most dangerous animal is the hippopotamus. First of all, it is a very powerful animal. It grows up to three meters in length, can weigh over three tonnes, and can outrun a human. It also has extremely powerful jaws that can easily bite a person in half. Secondly, the hippopotamus is very bad tempered. Anyone who gets in between an adult hippopotamus and its calf or the water is likely to be attacked. Finally, the hippopotamus is responsible for more than 500 deaths each year, which is more than any other large African animal. In conclusion, the power, temperament, and number of victims of the hippopotamus make it the most feared animal in Africa.

» The Topic Sentence

What is a topic sentence? The topic sentence can be seen as the key to your paragraph. It is the most important part of the paragraph, and it opens the door to your opinions or ideas about the topic. It gives the reader the main idea and must clearly state what the paragraph is about. As it is usually the first sentence, it must also catch the reader's attention.

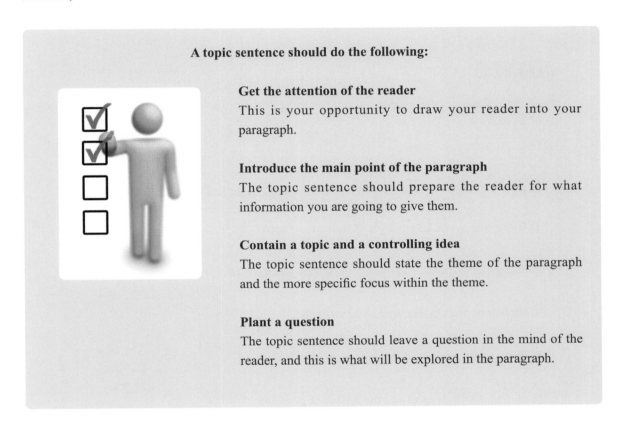

A topic sentence should do the following:

Get the attention of the reader
This is your opportunity to draw your reader into your paragraph.

Introduce the main point of the paragraph
The topic sentence should prepare the reader for what information you are going to give them.

Contain a topic and a controlling idea
The topic sentence should state the theme of the paragraph and the more specific focus within the theme.

Plant a question
The topic sentence should leave a question in the mind of the reader, and this is what will be explored in the paragraph.

A topic sentence has a topic and controlling idea. The topic is the thing being written about, and the controlling idea is the angle or point of focus.

Topic	Controlling idea

Example 1: Apoptosis, or programmed cell death, **has three qualities that make it a potential treatment for cancer.**

Example 2: Despite their similar appearance, there are **several important differences** between **tomato sauce and red pepper paste.**

Topics

Activity 1

Read the following topic sentences, put the topic in parentheses, and underline the controlling idea.

Example: (Brunel) revolutionized civil engineering through three landmark projects.

1) There are several advantages of learning to cook.

2) In the winter, people can avoid injuries by taking certain precautions.

3) My fear of dogs began when I was a child.

4) There are several disadvantages to online shopping.

5) My vacation in Hawaii was the best time of my life.

What Makes a Good Topic Sentence?

While there is some variation in how writers construct topic sentences, there are some general principles which are often followed.

1. It is a complete idea.

Good example:
Veganism benefits the environment in three ways.

Poor example: An incomplete sentence
There are many benefits.

2. It states a point that needs to be explained or proven.

Good example:
YX's revolutionary new computer is the best on the market.

Poor example: A simple fact
YX developed a new computer.

3. It has one direction.

Good example:
The college entrance exam should be reformed in three specific ways.

Bad example: Two controlling ideas
The college entrance system has benefits and disadvantages.

4. It has an appropriate focus.

Good example:
Social media appears to be causing serious mental health issues for many young people.

Poor example: Too specific
Social media is damaging for young people because it promotes online over offline relationships, contributes to an unhealthy body image, and leads to cyberbullying.

Poor example: Too broad
Since the beginning of time, communication has been essential.

Activity 2

Look at the following topic sentences. For each one, state whether it is a good topic sentence or a poor one and explain why.

Example: It happened years ago when we lived on Stanford Road.
Poor topic sentence. No topic.

1. Ostriches are birds.

_____

2. Hiking is one of the best types of exercise.

_____

3. There are three steps to take.

_____

4. What should be done about unemployment?

_____

5. The government should provide a basic income subsidy for all university students.

_____

6. These days, English education is a hot topic in Korea.

_____

7. English is both an easy and difficult language.

_____

8. There are many similarities between the United States and the United Kingdom.

_____

9. In Korea, people do not need a license to ride a bicycle.

_____

10. Steve Jobs's success came from the good decisions he made early in his career.

_____

Signpost Unlike direct thesis statements, topic sentences do not usually preview the supporting details. For more information about thesis statements, see page 55.

Activity 3

Read the following paragraph and select the most appropriate topic sentence from the list below.

Peterborough

Topic sentence: _____

First, Peterborough is known for Flagg Fen, which is an ancient Bronze Age settlement. The old town, which dates back to 1365 BCE, is one of the most important places in the country for studying ancient civilizations. The next historical site is Longthorpe, a picturesque village which features a Roman fort from the first century CE. The buildings in the village are all very old and traditional, yet they are all still lived in today. The third and most famous ancient structure is Peterborough Cathedral. Its origins can be traced back to 655 CE, and it has been used as a place of worship since then. The imposing Early English Gothic West Front was built in the 12th century and, with its three huge arches, is unique in style and a very impressive sight. In conclusion, Peterborough's historic sites make it an interesting and important city.

a. Prince William lives in Peterborough, England.

b. The City of Peterborough, England, is known for several historic features.

c. It is a famous city with many old buildings.

d. Let me introduce my hometown, which is old, beautiful, and fantastic.

Activity 4

Create topic sentences for the topics below.

Smoking

_____

Military service

_____

Blood donation

_____

The Introduction Sentence

The first sentence in a paragraph is usually the topic sentence. However, writers sometimes use the opening one or two (or more) sentences to provide background information. Like the topic sentence, the introduction sentence is usually more general than the supporting sentences. Unlike the topic sentence, the introduction sentence is not referred to in or supported by the supporting sentences. In most cases, the introduction sentence gives a general point to introduce the topic and then the topic sentence introduces the main idea which is not mentioned in the introduction sentence.

Activity 5

Read the paragraph below and identify the introduction sentence and the topic sentence.

Africa's Most Dangerous Animal

Africa is a large continent that is well known for its diverse and often dangerous wildlife. Surprisingly, the animal that is considered the most dangerous is the hippopotamus. First of all, the hippopotamus is a very powerful animal. It grows up to three meters in length, can weigh over three tonnes, and can outrun a human. It also has extremely powerful jaws that can easily bite a person in half. Secondly, the hippopotamus is very bad tempered. Anyone who gets in between an adult hippopotamus and its calf or the water is likely to be attacked. Finally, the hippopotamus is responsible for more than 500 deaths each year, which is more than any other large African animal. In conclusion the power, temperament, and number of victims of the hippopotamus make it the most feared animal in Africa.

Activity 6

Write one or two introduction sentences to give background information that will introduce each of the following topic sentences.

Introduction sentence: _____

_____

Topic sentence: Soccer is the greatest team sport in the world.

Introduction sentence: _____

_____

Topic sentence: There are three key steps to a flawless complexion.

» Supporting Sentences

In academic writing, it is necessary for the writer to provide support for their ideas. This might well require research and investigation on the part of the writer in order to gather sufficient support. The supporting information in a paragraph is given in the supporting sentences, the sentences that follow the topic sentence. They should always relate to the topic and back up the main idea.

Example: Topic sentence: My cat has three annoying habits.
1. Sleeping on me
2. Shedding fur
3. Leaving dead rodents under the refrigerator

Activity 1

Read the following paragraph and complete the exercises.

Fast Food Phobia

Fast food, particularly McDonald's, is an easy target for people who claim to care about health. However, there are good reasons to believe that McDonald's is not just a dietary evil. First of all, there is the assumption that McDonald's meals are fattening due to the high calorie content. In fact, according to a study by Queen's College in London, "A Big Mac contains just 510 calories, which is some way short of the recommended daily intake of 2,550 calories for men and 1,940 calories for women. Even the most calorific item on the menu, the Double Quarter Pounder with Cheese, only contains 740 calories" (17). The second common criticism leveled at McDonald's is the level of trans-fats. In reality, all meat contains trans-fats, so the same criticism must also be aimed at every restaurant with meat on their menu. McDonald's burgers contain about 1.5g per serving, which is just 8% of the daily limit recommended by the World Health Organization (23). Finally, the salt, or more specifically, sodium content of McDonald's meals is often attacked as a major health problem. The data shows this criticism is unjustified. The recommended daily intake of sodium for an adult is 1,500mg, and no more than 2,300mg. A Big Mac, McDonald's most famous and popular burger, contains just 1,040mg of sodium (12), which is well within the healthy limit. In summary, as with any other food, McDonald's can be part of a healthy diet as long as it is eaten in moderation.

1. Underline the topic sentence.

2. What are the three supporting ideas?

a) _____

_____

_____

b) _____

_____

_____

c) _____

_____

_____

Activity 2

Add ideas to support each of the following topic sentences.

There are three important components to the perfect date.

1. _____

2. _____

3. _____

There are several economic advantages to hosting the Olympic Games.

1. _____

2. _____

3. _____

A monarchy serves important functions.

1. _____

2. _____

3. _____

Evidence and Support

Each supporting sentence contains an idea that supports the topic sentence, along with supporting details or evidence to back up the idea. Supporting details are given in the form of examples, statistics, and quotations.

Examples

Examples are the easiest and most common supporting details. They are useful for adding interesting support to a paragraph and do not usually require as much research as quotes and statistics.

Example: Psychology graduates learn a range of skills that are desired by many employers, such as numerical and statistical skills, effective communication skills, and teamwork.

Statistics

Statistics are a good way of giving specific details using numbers. They can be very strong support for a point and can provide detailed and even surprising information.

Example: According to Professor Keeley at Newcastle University 28.7% of psychology graduates are attracted to accountancy, banking, and management, which are growth areas, compared with just 14% of IT graduates (Stubbs 2).

Quotations

Quotations are using the words of a respected authority on a subject to add support or credibility to your point. They are useful because they show the reader that your ideas are in line with those of experts in the field, and are therefore likely to be correct.

Example: According to Dr. Uffindel of the Bright Network, "It is true that these students know that if they want to apply their psychology theory in the workplace for a range of careers, they understand a period of further study and work experience-up to 12 months is necessary" (1).

Activity 3

Read the paragraph. Identify the relevant supporting sentences. What kind of support does the writer use? Underline any examples, statistics, and quotations.

The Most Employable Degree

A 2010 study showed that unemployment among recent graduates was at its highest since 1993 at 8.9% (BBC News). However, among the most successful were psychology graduates due to the skills learned, flexibility of the qualification, and practical experience gained on the course. Psychology graduates learn a range of skills that are desired by many employers, such as numerical and statistical skills, effective communication skills, and teamwork. Second, psychology graduates are often drawn to industries with more vacancies. According to Professor Keeley at Newcastle University, 28.7% of psychology graduates are attracted to accountancy, banking and management, which are growth areas, compared with just 14% of IT graduates (Stubbs 2). Finally, it is common for psychology students to gain practical experience in the workplace prior to graduation. According to Dr. Uffindell of the Bright Network, "It is true that these students know that if they want to apply their psychology theory in the workplace for a range of careers, they understand a period of further study and work experience–up to 12 months–is necessary" (1). Therefore, the skills, versatility, and experience gained by psychology graduates makes them comparatively successful in the job market.

Activity 4

Read the paragraph about McDonald's again and summarize the supporting details in the appropriate box.

Example:

Statistic:

Quotation:

Activity 5

Write a topic sentence on the following topics and give three supporting details.

Sport	Fashion	University

Topic sentence:

_____

Supporting details:

_____

_____

_____

_____

Topic sentence:

_____

Supporting details:

_____

_____

_____

_____

Topic sentence:

_____

Supporting details:

_____

_____

_____

_____

Unity

It is important that all of the supporting sentences in a paragraph match the topic sentence. This means that they should relate to both the topic and the controlling idea. If you are writing a paragraph about the life of Joseph Merrick, then all the supporting sentences should relate directly to the life of Joseph Merrick. Furthermore, each supporting sentence should relate to a single aspect of his life. We should not have sentences that focus on the romantic relationships of Joseph Merrick's sister, or on the pets of Joseph Merrick.

There are two common problems relating to unity in paragraphs.
1. The paragraph contains sentences relating to more than one topic.
2. The paragraph contains sentences supporting more than one controlling idea.

 Tip

For a cohesive paragraph, repeat the key nouns throughout the paragraph. You can also use synonyms to keep the cohesion but add variety.

Activity 6

Read the paragraph below and identify the sentence that does not match the topic sentence. Does the paragraph contain a) more than one topic, or b) more than one controlling idea?

The Difficult Life of Joseph Merrick

Life in 1860s London was tough, but it was particularly difficult for "Elephant Man" Joseph Merrick. Merrick is one of a number of famous disabled people to have a film made about their extraordinary life, along with Cristy Brown (*My Left Foot*, 1989) and Rocky Dennis (*Mask*, 1985). Merrick was born with a severe growth problem meaning that bones on the right side of his body, including skull, ribs, arm, and leg, continued to grow throughout his life. This led to respiratory problems, speech impediments, and, most notably, a physically repulsive appearance. After being abandoned as a child, Merrick was picked up by a backstreet sideshow, where he was cruelly treated by the owner who made money from showing his unusual exhibit to a paying public. Merrick was treated as an animal, and it was assumed from his appearance that he was unintelligent. Eventually, he was rescued by Dr. Fredrick Treves, and they built a relationship together. Dr. Treves studied Merrick's condition but could not cure him. Merrick's condition continued to deteriorate and at the age of 27 he died in his sleep. In conclusion, Joseph Merrick's remarkable story reminds us that there is a person behind every face.

Activity 7

Read the paragraph, and identify the sentence that does not match the topic sentence. Does the paragraph contain a) two topics, or b) more than one controlling idea?

Ancient Seoul

Seoul, the capital of South Korea, has a number of historical sites. The most famous is Gyeongbok Palace, which was the residence of the monarchy until Emperor Yunghui (Sunjong) was dethroned during the Japanese occupation in 1910. Gyeongbok Palace was originally built in 1394 as one of the five great palaces of the Joseon Dynasty and is located in the center of the city. The second famous historical site in Seoul is Joggye Temple (Jogyesa), which has been a place of worship for over 600 years. It is located close to Gyeongbok Palace in the center of Seoul. Gyeongju, the capital of Shilla Dynasty, also contains many historical sites including the distinctive dome-shaped tombs in which the remains of ancient rulers are buried. Another historical site in Seoul is the ancient fortress wall that was built to protect Hanyang, the capital of the Joseon Dynasty. The wall surrounds four mountains, Naksan, Namsan, Bugaksan, and Inwangsan and served to protect the city from invasions. In summary, these are just a few examples of the many historical sites in Seoul.

Connecting Words

Connecting words can be used to show the structure of a paragraph by indicating transitions from one supporting point to another. The table below shows some possible transition signal words and phrases.

Connecting Words and Phrases	
First, First of all, The first …, To begin with	The first idea in a series or sequence
Second, Secondly …	The second idea in a series or sequence
Third, Thirdly …	The third idea in a series or sequence
Next, Then, After that	The next idea in a series
In addition, Furthermore, Moreover	Making a further point
Similarly, Likewise	Comparing a similar idea
In contrast, On the other hand	Showing an opposing idea
Nevertheless	
Soon, Eventually	A transition over time in a time order paragraph

Activity 8

Read the paragraphs about ancient Seoul and Joseph Merrick once more and identify the connecting words and phrases.

Activity 9

Use the facts in the box below to create a series of supporting sentences on the topic below. Write a topic sentence to which all of your supporting sentences relate.

Ben Folds Five Facts

Career: Formed in 1993, broke up in 2000

Albums and chart success: *Ben Folds Five* (1995), did not chart in US Billboard 200

Whatever and Ever Amen (1997), reached no. 42 in US Billboard 200

The Unauthorized Biography of Reinhold Messner (1999), reached no. 35 in US Billboard 200

Members: Ben Folds (piano, vocals), Robert Sledge (bass guitar, vocals), Darren Jessee (drums, vocals)

From: North Carolina, USA

Most successful single: "Brick" (1997), reached no.19 in US Hot 100 Billboard Chart

Genre: Alternative rock

Known for: No guitar, songs that tell stories

Topic: _____

Title: _____

Topic sentence:

_____

Supporting sentences: _____

_____

_____

_____

_____

_____

_____

Activity 10

Now do the same but with details from your own research.

Topic: _____

Title: _____

Topic sentence:

_____

_____

_____

_____

Supporting sentences:

_____

_____

_____

_____

_____

_____

_____

_____

_____

_____

_____

_____

_____

_____

_____

_____

» The Concluding Sentence

The concluding sentence is the final sentence in a paragraph. It finishes the paragraph in a satisfying way, and it helps the reader to cement their understanding of the ideas.

A concluding sentence should do the following:

Signal the end of the paragraph

Start your concluding sentence with a transition expressing summation or effect to show readers they have reached the end of the paragraph.

Reinforce the main point of the paragraph

A concluding sentence needs to make reference to the topic of the paragraph and emphasize the point the author is trying to make.

Use new words

You should not simply cut and paste your topic sentence. Even when writers decide to restate the topic sentence, they need to paraphrase (change the words and change the order).

Stay on topic

A concluding sentence should not introduce new information to the paragraph, and writers should not leave personal notes to readers such as "Thank you for reading."

What Makes a Good Concluding Sentence?

Most paragraphs end with a concluding sentence. This sentence either reinforces the main idea or leaves readers with a related thought. All concluding sentences need to include the following:

1. Signal the end of the paragraph.

Begin your sentence with either a summation or an effect transition to indicate the end of the paragraph.

Summation	In conclusion	**Effect**	Therefore
	To sum up		Thus
	In summary		As a result
	To summarize		Consequently
	In brief		The evidence shows that
	In short		It is clear that

2. Conclude the paragraph in one of four ways.

The way that the paragraph ends depends on the type of paragraph. For example, a persuasive paragraph might end with a suggestion, but a paragraph about a historical figure will rarely end with a prediction about the future.

a. Restate the topic sentence.

(Paraphrase the topic and controlling idea to reinforce the basic point of the paragraph)

Topic Sentence: People love cats for their many endearing qualities.
Concluding Sentence: Therefore, people feel great affection for cats because of their appealing characteristics.

b. Restate the topic sentence and three major details.

(Paraphrase the main points of the paragraph to reinforce the main message)

Concluding Sentence: In conclusion, people feel great affection for cats because of their devotion, cleverness, and friendliness.

c. Make a related suggestion.

(Suggest a course of action to the reader based on the point of the paragraph)

Concluding Sentence: In summary, if people want an animal with an interesting personality, they should get a cat.

d. Make a related prediction.

(Write something that will happen in the near future based on the basic point of the paragraph)

Concluding Sentence: As a result, people will fall in love with cats' appealing characteristics if they own one.

 Tip

Do not put any new information in your concluding sentence.

Do not leave a personal message to the reader.

Activity 1

Read the following paragraph and use what you have learned so far to select the most appropriate concluding sentence from the options.

Ig Nobels

The Ig Nobels, an event that recognizes ingenuity in science research, is an awards ceremony like no other. The awards ceremony is organized by Annals of Improbable Research (AIR), which is a humor magazine presented as a parody of serious scientific literature. The self-stated aim of the Ig Nobels is "first make people laugh, and then make them think." Each year in October, scientists gather for the annual Ig Nobel awards ceremony, held at Harvard University, to see prizes distributed by genuine Nobel Prize winners. As with many awards ceremonies, the Ig Nobel prize winners are expected to make a speech, and the organizers have implemented an unusual but effective method for keeping these speeches from going on for too long. Miss Sweety Poo is a young girl who sits on the stage and as soon as she is tired of a speech repeats, "Please stop: I'm bored," until the speaker leaves the stage. While the ceremony is known for rewarding unusual research, there is often a use for the findings. For example, a study showing that malaria mosquitoes are attracted to the smell of human feet, and also, Limburger cheese has led to the development of effective mosquito traps. However, bad science is also recognized and rewarded as a criticism, such as with Jacques Benveniste. Benveniste's research "proved" that water has a memory, and that this information can be transmitted over the Internet.

_____

_____

a) While science is often seen as serious, the Ig Nobels give a more lighthearted angle focused on humor and entertainment.

b) In summary, the Ig Nobel awards are the biggest prizes in the science community.

c) In conclusion, the Ig Nobels are an unusual ceremony that began in 1991.

d) Furthermore, the unusual nature of the Ig Nobel awards makes them one of the highlights of the science calendar.

Types of Summary Concluding Sentences

There are two main types of concluding sentences that summarize the paragraph. The first is a summary of the main points of the paragraph while the second restates the topic sentence in different words.

Activity 2

Read the paragraph about the evolution of snakes.

1. Identify the topic sentence.

2. Identify the supporting details. How do they support the topic sentence?
   Then read the two example concluding sentences and identify which one is a summary of the main points of the paragraph and which is a restatement of the topic sentence.

Legless

Occasionally venomous, often depicted as cunning or deceitful, one thing that all snakes have in common is, besides their tail, an obvious absence of limbs. However, the evidence suggests that this has not always been the case. Experts believe that all lizards and snakes evolved from a reptilian common ancestor. Fossil evidence from the Cretaceous Period (144–65 million years ago) reveals at least four genera of early snakes: three in the Middle East and one in South America. The unusual feature of these snake fossils is the presence of short hind legs. These early snakes evolved from burrowing lizards with short and stubby limbs, and streamlined bodies. Over time, the front legs regressed until they were just short vestigial stumps. Fossils of primitive species, such as boas and pythons, still have these vestigial stumps as evidence of their legged ancestors. These are known as anal spurs and are used to grip during mating. Other modern snake species have lost even these traces of their lizard heritage. Genetic evidence reveals that evolution in Hox genes, which are responsible for limb development, resulted in the dramatic reduction on limb size and the eventual loss of functioning front and hind limbs in all modern snakes.

_____

_____

Concluding sentence 1: In conclusion, various lines of evidence show that primitive snakes had legs.

Concluding sentence 2: It is clear from fossil evidence, the anatomy of primitive modern snake species, and genetic analysis, that legless modern snakes evolved from legged ancestors.

Activity 3

There are four main steps in the process of writing a concluding sentence.

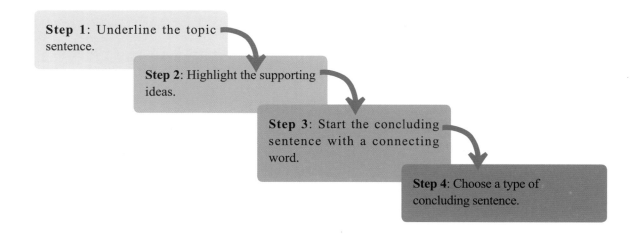

Step 1: Underline the topic sentence.

Step 2: Highlight the supporting ideas.

Step 3: Start the concluding sentence with a connecting word.

Step 4: Choose a type of concluding sentence.

Choosing a Pet

There are a number of things to consider when choosing a pet. Most importantly, people must carefully consider whether or not they are really ready to take on the responsibility of caring for an animal. Can they provide a pet with everything it will need in order to live a happy life in their care? Once someone is sure they can handle a pet, they must think about what they want from their pet. Fish look beautiful and are not too demanding in terms of time and space, but some consider them boring. Dogs and cats can be playful, affectionate, and can become great companions. Hamsters are popular and cute, but they are nocturnal. Some people want a more unusual pet, such as a lizard or an axolotl which need specialist equipment and knowledge. Finally, anyone thinking of buying a pet must consider what they are able to offer their animal. For someone with ample time and space, a dog might be a great option since they need exercise and attention. For someone who has never kept a pet before, it might be a good idea to start with a rabbit, which does not require training and does not live as long. It is irresponsible to get a pet which people cannot care for adequately.

Concluding sentence:

_____

_____

Activity 4

Read the following topic sentences from paragraphs elsewhere in the chapter, and rewrite them as concluding sentences.

Seoul, the capital of South Korea, has a number of historical sites.

_____

_____

_____

_____

Life in 1860s London was tough, but it was particularly difficult for "Elephant Man" Joseph Merrick.

_____

_____

_____

_____

Among the most successful were psychology graduates due to the skills learned, flexibility of the qualification, and practical experience gained on the course.

_____

_____

_____

_____

There are good reasons to believe that McDonald's is not just a dietary evil.

_____

_____

_____

_____

_____

» Paragraph Outlines

An outline is a useful stage of the planning process in any kind of academic or formal writing, including paragraphs, essays, and reports. It helps you to arrange your ideas in a logical way, and it makes the process of writing your final piece far simpler.

Topic: International Marriage

Topic sentence: In an increasingly globalized society, it is easier than ever before to meet people of other nationalities, and for the benefits to society, international couples, and their children, people should pursue intercultural romance and marriage.

Supporting detail 1: International marriage benefits the couple.

Supporting detail 2: International marriages will benefit society in the long term.

Supporting detail 3: International marriage benefits the children.

Concluding sentence: International relationships should be strongly encouraged.

Activity 1

Here are the components of an outline for a paragraph about yoga. Put them into a logical order by matching them with the relevant paragraph sections.

a. The Benefits of Yoga

b. Develops clear thinking, improves concentration.

c. Physical benefits.

d. Reduces fear, anger and worry, helps you to feel calm, develops self-confidence.

e. Mental benefits.

f. Improves blood circulation, improves digestion, makes you strong and flexible.

g. Emotional benefits.

h. Therefore, to build mental, physical and emotional health, consider practicing yoga.

i. Practicing yoga regularly can be good for your mind, your body and your emotions.

1. Topic _____a_____

2. Topic sentence: _____

3. Supporting point 1: _____

4. Detail: _____

5. Supporting point 2: _____

6. Detail: _____

7. Supporting point 3: _____

8. Detail: _____

9. Concluding sentence: _____

Once the supporting points have been arranged in a logical order, you can begin to add details. At this point your paragraph really begins to take shape.

Topic: International Marriage

Topic sentence: In an increasingly globalized society, it is easier than ever before to meet people of other nationalities, and for the benefits to society, international couples, and their children, people should pursue intercultural romance and marriage.

Supporting detail 1: International marriage benefits the couple directly. The couple can learn each other's language and culture, as well as enjoy frequent travel opportunities.

Supporting detail 2: International marriages will benefit society in the long term. John Giddings, a professor at Oxford University, suggests that intermarriage leads to greater genetic diversity, which could improve herd immunity in future generations.

Supporting detail 3: International marriage benefits the children. Children of international parents have the advantage of identifying with two cultures, leading to more rounded opinions and richer life experience.

Concluding sentence: International relationships are nothing new and for the good of couples, society, and children, they should be strongly encouraged.

Activity 2

Add controlling ideas to the following topics to form topic sentences then add three supporting points.

Popular Foreign Food

Topic sentence:

_____

_____

Support 1: _____

Support 2: _____

Support 3: _____

Future Technology

Topic sentence:

_____

_____

Support 1: _____

Support 2: _____

Support 3: _____

Travel Experience

Topic sentence:

_____

_____

Support 1: _____

Support 2: _____

Support 3: _____

Activity 3

Choose one of the topics from Activity 2 and develop it into a paragraph outline.

Topic: _____

_____

Topic sentence: _____

_____

a) Supporting detail 1:

_____

_____

_____

b) Supporting detail 2:

_____

_____

_____

c) Supporting detail 3:

_____

_____

_____

Concluding sentence:

_____

_____

_____

_____

_____

Activity 4

Write a paragraph about one of the topics below within 30 minutes. Start by brainstorming to gather and develop your ideas. Write an outline including a topic sentence, supporting details and a concluding sentence. Finally, write your paragraph.

Hometown	Disaster	Hobby

Plan your time: When writing within a time limit it is very important that you plan your time effectively. Here is a suggestion for planning your time for this writing task.

Brainstorm	5 minutes
Outline	7 minutes
Paragraph	15 minutes
Check	3 minutes

Paragraph checklist: Does your paragraph include the following:

Title	____
Format (see page 8)	____
Topic sentence	____
Relevant supporting details	____
Concluding sentence	____

Activity 5

Using what you have learned so far, write a paragraph on one of the topics below.

An interesting instrument	A common superstition
The perfect partner	A hero
A successful company	Technology of tomorrow

» Essay Structure

There are three main parts to a five-paragraph essay. The first part is called the introduction, and it is a single paragraph. The second is the body. In a five-paragraph essay, the body is made up of three paragraphs. The final part of the essay is the conclusion, which like the introduction is a single paragraph. Look at the following chart to see how a paragraph and an essay are structured.

Paragraph	Essay
Topic sentence	**Introduction paragraph** • Hook • Background information • Thesis statement
A. Supporting detail	**Body paragraph 1** • Topic sentence • Supporting details • Concluding sentence
B. Supporting detail	**Body paragraph 2** • Topic sentence • Supporting details • Concluding sentence
C. Supporting detail	**Body paragraph 3** • Topic sentence • Supporting details • Concluding sentence
Concluding sentence	**Conclusion paragraph** • Restate overview • Summarize main points • Conclude memorably

Essay Example

Complete the following questions on "stress."

1. Life is full of stressful events (stressors). What causes you stress?

_____

_____

_____

2. When you are stressed, how do you feel physically? What changes happen to you during times of stress? Check the physical symptoms that happen to you.

__ increased heart rate	__ hair loss	__ sweaty hands/palms
__ feeling irritable	__ muscle tension	__ shoulder or neck pain
__ headaches	__ dry mouth	__ butterflies in the stomach
__ skin irritations	__ insomnia	__ indigestion
__ shortness of breath	__ depression	__ feelings of anxiety

Responding to Stress

The term "stress" is often used to describe feelings of being overloaded and overwhelmed with the changes and demands of life. **Sheldon Cohen et al**, in their book *Measuring Stress*, describe stress **as the process in which "environmental demands tax or exceed the adaptive capacity of an organism, resulting in psychological and biological changes" (3).** These biological changes may be immediate and temporal, as well as, long term and constant and can have both positive and negative effects. *When examining the effects of stress on the body, it is common to discuss three biological responses: the hormonal response, the cardiovascular response, and the immune response.*

During times of emotional or physical stress, hormones are released into the circulatory system, resulting in a number of metabolic changes. **For example**, the release of hormones, such as epinephrine, norepinephrine, and dopamine are found to increase arousal and neural stimulation. When the body senses danger or a threat, the release of hormones by the adrenal medulla in the kidneys help to prepare a person to either fight or run away. The fight-or-flight response is a natural reaction to external threats or stress and has a number of beneficial effects, such as increasing muscular tension, and increasing alertness and awareness. While the fight-or-flight response can be advantageous in certain contexts, it can also inhibit performance in others. When concentration is needed, such as during exams or before giving a presentation, hormone release may actually reduce performance by suppressing short-term memory. *In terms of the effect of hormone release on the body, it is a significant factor influencing biological change.*

In addition to a hormonal response caused by stress, there is also a cardiovascular response triggered by neural and hormonal influences. Changes in heart rate, blood pressure and peripheral blood flow occur as a result of a release of hormones into the bloodstream and the activation of the autonomic nervous system. **Dr. David Engel, a cardiologist at Samsung Medical Center,** describes the cardiovascular response as "non-specific" meaning that different stressors or tasks affect the cardiovascular system and indeed people, in different ways **(77)**. For example, in a study by **Benschop et al**., men tend to experience changes in blood pressure, whereas women tended to display an increase in cardiac output and heart rate in response to severe stress **(290)**. During times of stress, heart rate can increase dramatically from a resting rate of about 70-80 beats per minute to over 150 beats per minute and vasoconstriction (narrowing of the blood vessels) results in an increase in blood pressure. *Changes to the cardiovascular system are one of the most easily recognizable effects to life's stresses.*

Finally, stress, particularly prolonged or persistent stress, may have a negative effect on the immune system. The immune system is the body's natural defense system that protects the body against foreign bodies (antigens), such as viruses. When the immune system is weakened, the ability of the body to fight disease is compromised. Stressors also result in a release of another type of hormone: corticosteroids. Corticosteroids are a class of hormones that reduce the effectiveness of the immune system to deal with foreign bodies by reducing the number of white blood cells, lymphocytes, which help the body to fight infections. Research also suggests that there may be a connection between continual stress and disease. Studies by **Cohen et al**., and **Levy et al**., reported higher rates of cancer and infections in stressed populations. *While the debate regarding stress and immunology will no doubt continue, many people assert that reducing stress is a first important step towards maintaining a healthy body.*

In conclusion, stress is an unavoidable part of life and can have both detrimental and beneficial effects on performance and health. The feeling of being stressed is not only a psychological response to a condition or context but a biological reaction that is easily measureable. When stressed, people may exhibit an urge to escape or face a situation head on as the hormonal response kicks in. A pounding heart and heightened blood pressure are the first tell-tale signs of stress. Finally, while stressful feelings may subside as quickly as they came, if left unattended, health and vitality may be reduced and the risk of disease may increase. As stress becomes a more common and permanent feature in the lives of many people, understanding its effect on the body is essential in order to combat its negative effects.

Activity 2

Go back through the essay and look at the parts of the essay that are highlighted. These highlighted parts are important components of an academic essay and will be explained in this section of the book.

» The Introductory Paragraph

The introductory paragraph in an essay does three things:

1. **Introduce the topic**

2. **Show the structure of the essay**, often with the major sections of the essay or its structural principle clearly stated.

3. **State the thesis of the essay**, preferably in a single statement with a clear main clause.

The introductory paragraph consists of three parts:

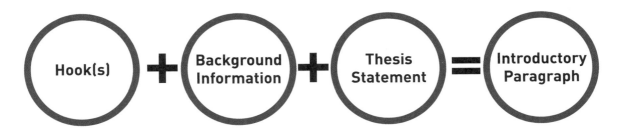

What Is a Thesis Statement?

The thesis statement is a road map for the essay; it tells the reader what to expect from the rest of the essay.

The thesis statement is similar to a topic sentence in that it serves to control or shape the text. The thesis statement, like a topic sentence, contains a **topic** (T) and **controlling idea(s)** (CI). However, with the thesis statement, the T and CI influence the whole essay.

In this sense, a thesis statement is like a "super-topic sentence."

There are some differences, however, between a topic sentence and a thesis statement:
- A thesis statement is usually the **final sentence** in the introductory paragraph
- A thesis statement may list subtopics, which are smaller topics that relate to the main topic that will be expanded upon in the body paragraphs

Direct and Indirect Thesis Statements

A thesis statement can be direct or indirect. A direct thesis statement contains subtopics and therefore gives a specific outline of the essay.

Indirect thesis statement	There are considerable benefits of learning English for Korean students.
Direct thesis statement	For Korean people, learning English is important for three reasons: to gain entrance to good universities, improve job prospects, and open social opportunities.

Direct Thesis Statement

Example: In order for Sungkyunkwan University to become the leading university in Korea, three areas need to be reformed: the university **scholarship and welfare system**, the **administrative system**, and the **system of hiring faculty**.

This sentence tells the reader what the essay is going to be about (i.e. what Sungkyunkwan University needs to do to become the best university in Korea) and provides a structural outline for the body paragraphs.

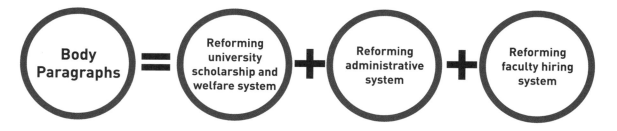

Activity 1

Read the following introduction, and answer the questions.

Today, smoking is an issue that is on everybody's mind. The whole country is divided on this issue. Some people believe that smoking should be banned everywhere while others are not so harsh. While it is true that smokers have rights too, tobacco should be outlawed because smoking endangers everyone's health, pollutes the environment, and drains people of valuable energy.

1. What is the thesis statement? Underline it.

2. How many subtopics are there? Underline them.

3. What do you think the rest of the essay will be about?

    a. The history of tobacco

    b. Why smoking is a bad habit

    c. Why tobacco should be banned (prohibited)

    d. How smoking divides the country

💡 Punctuation Tip

Colons (:)

Colons are used to introduce a list of items. They can be particularly helpful when writing thesis statements because they allow the writer to introduce the subtopics. Colons must be preceded by an independent clause.

IC

Example: Living in a city has certain advantages over living in town: more employment opportunities, better medical facilities, and higher educational standards.^{colon}

Activity 2

Make the following into direct thesis statements by adding subtopics to them.

Computers are necessary for university students for three reasons

_____

_____

Successful K-pop groups have the following qualities

_____

_____

Students have a difficult time taking notes in class due to

_____

_____

To gain an internship in a prestigious Korean company requires

_____

_____

There are several reasons why the South Korean government should invest in education

_____

_____

There are three negative consequences for the population explosion in Seoul

_____

_____

Indirect Thesis Statement

An indirect thesis statement does not contain subtopics; however, the topic is still clearly stated.

Example: In order for Sungkyunkwan University to become the leading university in Korea, three areas need to be reformed.

What Makes a Good Thesis Statement?

A good thesis statement usually has at least one of the following attributes:

1. Takes a stance or position on a topic

Good example:
There are three reasons why smoking should be banned in all public places in Korea.

Poor example: **Does not give an opinion.**
A lot of people smoke in Korea.

2. Expresses one idea

Good example:
Shakespeare is considered one of the most influential figures in literary history.

Poor example: **Expresses more than one idea.**
Shakespeare is considered an important literary figure, and he was born in Stratford-upon-Avon which is a beautiful town in England.

3. It should be clear and specific

Good example:
Michael Jackson possessed all the qualities of a pop icon: incredible dancing skills, great vocal ability, and a commanding stage presence.

Poor example: **Is too broad.**
Michael Jackson is very famous.

4. Answers the question "Why?"

Good example: (Answers the question, "Why is the adoption rate in the United States increasing?)
Adoption rates in the United States are increasing due to incentive programs, positive campaigns, and fertility issues.

Poor example: **Does not answer "Why?"**
Researchers understand why the adoption rate in the United States is increasing.

Activity 3

Look at the following thesis statements. For each one, state whether it is a good thesis statement or a poor one. Give a reason for your view. If the thesis statement is poor, change it to make it better.

1. Learning English has some negative and positive aspects.

_____

_____

_____

2. Korean companies need to enhance new technologies to increase sales, and they also need to change their marketing strategies.

_____

_____

_____

3. There are many causes and effects of global warming.

_____

_____

_____

4. *Buchaechum*, a traditional Korean form of dance, is a vital part of Korean culture and should therefore be taught to all female high school students.

_____

_____

_____

5. Natural disasters, such as earthquakes and tsunamis, are something people should get used to.

_____

_____

_____

General Statements

Making a good first impression is important when writing the introductory paragraph. The opening statements in an introductory paragraph should help to capture the attention of the reader as well as introduce the general topic of the essay.

In the introductory paragraph, the general statements precede the thesis statement and are made up of devices called a "**hook**" and "**background information**."

Hook

A hook is an interesting statement that helps to engage the readers by capturing their attention. There are many different kinds of hooks that can be used to start an introduction. Be aware that not every type of hook will work for every style of writing.

1. Interesting fact

A surprising fact, figure, or statistic can be a great way to draw interest in the topic. It can help the reader to focus on your main essay idea and can serve as a bridge for further supporting details in the body.

> **Example**:
>
> The city of Seoul has seen massive population changes over the last century and now accounts for almost half of the population of South Korea. **It is estimated that the Seoul National Capital Area has around 25 million inhabitants and is second only behind Tokyo in terms of world metropolitan figures.** While this population boom has been a key reason for the economic development of Seoul, and indeed South Korea, it has also had negative effects. There are three main negative consequences of the population explosion in Seoul.

2. Setting the Scene

This type of hook uses descriptive language to create a "picture" for your reader. It may describe how someone or something looks, smells, feels, or tastes and is useful in helping the reader connect with the topic you will introduce.

> **Example**:
>
> **The buildings and houses lay scattered and in ruins. The night air is filled with the cries of people and the sirens of the emergency vehicles trying to navigate through the broken streets. People wander in a daze picking up personal items from the debris that used to be their houses.** The chaos and destruction is overwhelming and tells a story of the awesome power of nature. An earthquake has struck. Earthquakes are one of the most devastating forces known to humanity because of a number of terrifying effects: shaking and ground rupture, tsunamis, and soil liquefaction.

3. Question

Asking a question in the introductory paragraph can help create an attachment between the reader and the writer. To strengthen the effect of the question, it is better to avoid yes/no questions or directly ask the reader a question (Do you like chocolate? Do you know Kim, Tae Hee?). Writers are meant to answer questions for readers. Therefore, writers should only use thought provoking questions that help to transition from one section or point to another. In addition, questions should be used sparingly.

> **Example**:
>
> Today, in the United States of America, heart disease is the number one cause of death and a major cause of disability. It is estimated that about every 30 seconds, an American will have some kind of coronary event. A healthy lifestyle and diet are seen as the best weapons against heart disease and yet, for many Americans, confusion still exists regarding what they should or should not consume. Most people already know that reducing saturated and trans fatty acids is an important first step; however, **what other dietary choices should people make?** Surprisingly, recent research has shown that the following three beverages have an effect on reducing the risk of heart disease: coffee, red wine, and beer.

4. Definition

A definition hook is used when the writer wishes to explain a difficult or unknown term that will be used throughout the essay.

Example:

For many visitors in China, the sight of Chinese people sitting around a table thoughtfully placing small tiles on a board is as much a part of the Chinese experience as visiting the Great Wall. The animated discussions and sounds of slapping tiles are signs that an intense game of Mahjong is taking place. **Mahjong is a traditional Chinese board game commonly played by four people. It is played with 136 tiles based on Chinese characters and symbols, and the object is to build sets by drawing and discarding tiles.** Once positions at the table have been finalized, there are three important steps involved in playing Mahjong: dealing the tiles, drawing the tiles, and building and breaking the wall.

5. Anecdote

An anecdote is a short story or personal account of a person, place, incident, or event that can be used to illustrate the ideas you want to make in your essay. Anecdotes are usually interesting and amusing and are based on real incidences.

Example:

Every day as a young boy, Edison "Edson" Arantes do Nascimento would walk down to the local school with his friends and kick an old leather ball around the concrete playground. When alone and without a ball, a sock stuffed with old newspapers tied at the top would suffice. Playing barefoot while kicking an old sock around the streets of Sao Paulo, Brazil never seemed to trouble the young man. He dreamed of a greater future. Early life was not easy for the hopeful young soccer star, and yet through the desperation and the difficulties, Edison Arantes do Nascimento rose to the top to become the greatest soccer player of all: Pelé.

6. Funnel

This type of hook is like a funnel because it is wide at the top and narrow at the bottom. It starts with general opening statements about the topic and gradually becomes narrower and more focused. The funnel finishes with a specific statement that can lead the reader into the thesis statement.

Example:

According to research by the Organization for Economic Cooperation and Development (OECD), South Korea is now ranked third among OECD countries with respect to divorce (Lee 15). The surging divorce rate is of great concern to family planning and welfare organizations, and the government has now been pulled into the issue as the problems caused by divorce begin to escalate. In order to navigate through this social transition, an understanding of the causes of divorce should be examined. Perhaps then some solutions can be found. There are three main reasons that can account for the high divorce rate in modern Korean society: the change in women's status in society, shift from collectivism to individualism, and a change in values regarding divorce.

Activity 4

Go back through each example introductory paragraph and underline the thesis statement. Which ones are direct thesis statements? Which ones are indirect?

Direct: _____

Indirect: _____

Now look at the following thesis statements (ThS). For each one, add a hook(s).

1. _____

_____

_____

_____

_____

_____

_____

ThS: In most occupations, women are still unequal to men in three areas: salary, power, and status.

2. _____

_____

_____

_____

_____

_____

_____

ThS: Living in a dormitory offers several advantages to first-year students.

Choose two of the thesis statements from Activity 2, and add a hook(s).

3. _____

_____

_____

_____

_____

_____

_____

ThS: _____

4. _____

_____

_____

_____

_____

_____

_____

ThS: _____

Background Information

It is often necessary to provide some kind of bridge to connect the hook(s) and the thesis statement. Providing some background information helps the reader understand what the topic is about. Although it may appear from the flow diagram on page 54 that background information comes between the hook and the thesis statement, it can come before the hook, after the hook, or both. Together the two parts make up the general statements. Consider the following two examples.

Example 1:

    <u>The city of Seoul has seen massive population changes over the last century and now accounts for almost half of the population of South Korea.</u> **It is estimated that the Seoul National Capital Area has around 25 million inhabitants and is second only behind Tokyo in terms of world metropolitan figures.** <u>While this population boom has been a key reason for the economic development of Seoul, and indeed South Korea, it has also had negative effects as well.</u> There are three main negative consequences of the population explosion in Seoul.

The hook is in bold. The thesis statement is the last sentence. The underlined information serves to frame the hook and thesis statement. We call this background information.

In Example 2, there are two different kinds of hooks. What are they?

1. _____

2. _____

Example 2:

    In the United States of America today, heart disease is the number one cause of death and is a major cause of disability. It is estimated that about every 30 seconds, an American will have some kind of coronary event. A healthy lifestyle and diet is seen as the best weapons against heart disease and yet for many Americans, confusion still exists regarding what they should or should not consume. Most people already know that reducing saturated and trans fatty acids is an important first step; however, what other dietary choices should people make? Surprisingly, recent research has shown that the following three beverages have an effect on reducing the risk of heart disease: coffee, red wine, and beer.

Activity 5

Look at the following topics. For each one, write a clear thesis statement (either direct or indirect), and then add some general statements.

Topic: School examinations

_____

_____

_____

_____

_____

_____

_____

Topic: University

_____

_____

_____

_____

_____

_____

_____

Topic: Learning a language

_____

_____

_____

_____

_____

_____

_____

_____

The Body Paragraphs

In the five-paragraph model essay, the body consists of three paragraphs. Each paragraph develops a subdivision of the topic that is described in the thesis statement. Like supporting sentences in a paragraph, each body paragraph helps to develop and support the main idea of the essay.

Each body paragraph usually contains these three parts:

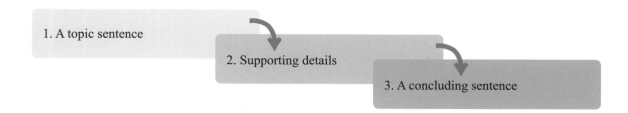

If you have used a direct thesis statement in your introductory paragraph, each subtopic will form the main theme in each body paragraph. Each main idea can then be examined and described in more detail. If you have used an indirect thesis statement, then suitable ideas will need to be created. This will usually take place during pre-writing and will form part of the essay outline.

Example:

Responding to Stress

The term "stress" is often used to describe the feelings of being overloaded and overwhelmed with the changes and demands of life. Sheldon Cohen et al, in their book *Measuring Stress*, describe stress as the process in which "environmental demands tax or exceed the adaptive capacity of an organism, resulting in psychological and biological changes" (3). These biological changes may be immediate and temporal as well as long term and constant, and can have both positive and negative effects. When measuring the effects of stress on the body, it is common to discuss three biological responses: the **hormonal response**, the **cardiovascular response**, and the **immune response**.

Body Patterns and Organization

Depending on the type of essay you are writing, different patterns or organizational structures are used. These patterns will be explained in more detail later in the book when you examine "Types of Writing." In the meantime, we will work on a basic 3–step paragraph structure.

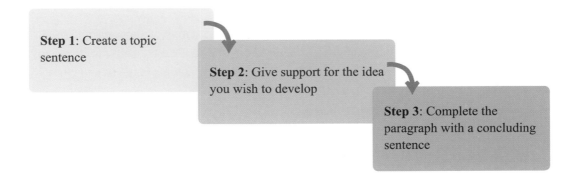

Step 1: Create a topic sentence

Step 2: Give support for the idea you wish to develop

Step 3: Complete the paragraph with a concluding sentence

Introductory paragraph	**Thesis statement**: When measuring the effects of stress on the body, it is common to discuss three biological responses: the **hormonal response**, the **cardiovascular response**, and the **immune response**.
B1: Hormonal response	• Clear topic sentence • Supporting details that discuss and/or provide evidence for **the hormonal response** • A clear concluding sentence
B2: Cardiovascular response	• Clear topic sentence • Supporting details that discuss and/or provide evidence for the **cardiovascular response** • A clear concluding sentence
B3: Immune response	• Clear topic sentence • Supporting details that discuss and/or provide evidence for **the immune response** • A clear concluding sentence
Concluding paragraph	• The explanation for concluding paragraphs begins on page 76

Supporting Details

The supporting details in each body paragraph must clearly relate to that paragraph's topic sentence. There are a number of different kinds of supporting details.

Description	Soil liquefaction commonly occurs during earthquakes and results in the soil losing its strength and stiffness. Consequently, it effectively turns into "quicksand," causing structural failures in towns and cities.
Definition	Soil liquefaction is defined as the transformation from a solid state to a liquid state as a consequence of increased pressure and stress (Gutani 138).
Examples	English is widely used by many Korean professors as the principal means of instruction. For example, according to Incheon University's website, 36% of Korean professors now use English in the classroom (Kim 29).
Statistics/figure	According to statistics from a recent Gallup poll, Korean parents in Seoul spend 200,000 won a month on average on private English tuition (Shirazi 3).
Fact	Sungkyunkwan University was founded in 1398 and is the oldest university in East Asia.
Quotation	On the topic of customer service, Rolf Bauer, Chief Executive of Neo Heavy Industry Korea (NHIK), said, "It is vital for our customers to understand that when we make a promise, we deliver" (Dennison 19).

Activity 6

For each of the following thesis statements, select one subtopic and provide supporting details.

1. Tobacco should be outlawed because smoking endangers everyone's health, pollutes the environment, and drains people of valuable energy.

Body idea: _____

Supporting details: _____

_____

_____

_____

_____

_____

2. Living in a city has certain advantages over living in a town: better entertainment options, greater employment opportunities, and more efficient transportation.

Body idea: _____

Supporting details: _____

_____

_____

_____

_____

_____

3. The computer gaming boom is a serious problem in South Korea for three reasons: it can lead to addiction, cause physical health problems, and lead to anti-social behavior.

Body idea: _____

Supporting details: _____

_____

_____

_____

_____

Activity 7

From the following indirect thesis statement, create three body paragraphs following the 3–step approach.

Step 1: Create a topic sentence

Step 2: Give support for the idea you wish to develop

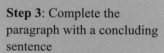

Step 3: Complete the paragraph with a concluding sentence

ThS: Living in a dormitory offers several advantages to first-year students.

B1 Topic sentence: _____

_____

_____

Supporting details: _____

_____

_____

_____

_____

_____

_____

_____

Concluding sentence: _____

_____

_____

_____

Body Paragraph Transitions

It was mentioned on page 35 that good writing must have unity. That is, the ideas in the paragraph should all support each other. In order to achieve unity across paragraphs, transitional words and phrases are necessary. Transition words are signposts that provide signals to the reader on the organizational structure of an essay.

When used in an essay, transitions usually precede the independent clause; thus, they are commonly found at the beginning of a body or concluding paragraph. Transition words are usually followed by a comma.

Example 1:
First, reforming the university scholarship and welfare system is a vital step in helping Sungkyunkwan University become a leader in education.
Second, reforming the administrative system is also very important.
Finally, changing the faculty hiring system is necessary to ensure that high standards are kept.

Example 2:
Reforming the university scholarship and welfare system is a vital step in helping Sungkyunkwan University become a leader in education.
In addition to reforming the scholarship and welfare system, changes to the administrative system are vitally important.
Lastly, a change to the faculty hiring system is necessary to ensure high standards are kept.

Common Transition Words

Transitions that indicate time or sequence	first, second, third, next, finally, lastly
Transitions that indicate more information	next, in addition, furthermore, similarly, in the same way, also, moreover
Transitional chains	• First..second..third • In the first place...also..lastly • In the first place...just the same way...finally

B2 Topic sentence: _____

_____

_____

Supporting details: _____

_____

_____

_____

_____

_____

_____

Concluding sentence: _____

_____

_____

B3 Topic sentence: _____

_____

_____

Supporting details: _____

_____

_____

_____

_____

_____

_____

Concluding sentence: _____

_____

_____

» The Concluding Paragraph

The final paragraph in an essay is the conclusion. Along with the introductory paragraph, it helps to frame your essay. In some respects, the concluding paragraph is like a mirror image of your introductory paragraph.

Introductory paragraph

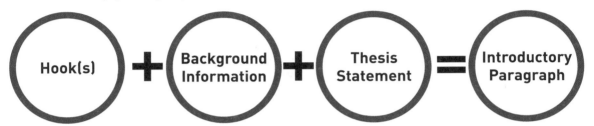

Concluding paragraph

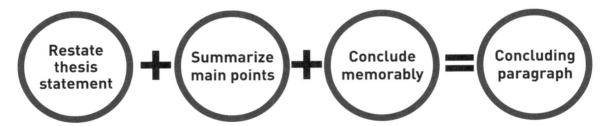

Like your body paragraphs, the concluding paragraph usually begins with a transition. Next, the writer **restates** the thesis statement found in the introductory paragraph and then **summarizes** the ideas in the main body. Finally, a **reverse hook** can be used to conclude memorably and to leave the reader with an interesting final thought.

Restating the Thesis Statement

By restating the thesis statement, the concluding paragraph can be connected to the introductory paragraph. We make this connection by paraphrasing the thesis statement.

Pages 216 - 221 cover paraphrasing and summarizing. The two basic rules for effective paraphrasing are:

1. Find synonyms
2. Change the sentence structure or word order

Example 1: James loves going to the mountains, but Sarah loves to swim.
1. James likes hiking, but Sarah enjoys swimming.
2. Sarah enjoys swimming, but James likes hiking.

Example 2: Thesis statement

Living in a large city has certain advantages over living in a small town: better entertainment options, greater employment opportunities, and more efficient transportation.

Restatement of the thesis statement:
1. It is better to live in a large city than a small town for the following reasons: more interesting things to do, greater job flexibility, easier to commute to places.
2. Citizens who live in large cities have more choices with regard to entertainment and culture. In addition, it is easier to get a job, and the transportation is more convenient. It is clear then, that living in a large city is better.

Activity 1

Rewrite the following thesis statements using the basic paraphrasing steps.

Earthquakes are one of the most devastating forces known to humanity because of a number of terrifying effects: shaking and ground rupture, tsunamis, and soil liquefaction.

_____

_____

_____

Signpost See page 216 for more information on paraphrasing.

Surprisingly, recent research has shown that the following three beverages have an effect on reducing the risk of heart attack: coffee, red wine, and beer.

_____

_____

_____

There are three important steps involved in playing Mahjong once positions at the table have been finalized: building and breaking the wall, dealing the tiles, and drawing the tiles.

_____

_____

_____

Summarizing the Main Points

If you have used an indirect thesis statement, a brief summary of the main points is recommended. This will remind the reader of the key ideas in your essay. Even if you have restated a direct thesis statement, a summary of the main points can still be worthwhile. You do not need to re–tell all the information; a few sentences are often enough.

Example:
ThS: There are three main negative consequences of the population explosion in Seoul.

B1: More traffic congestion and delays in travel

B2: An increase in air, soil, and noise pollution

B3: Increasing cost of living

In conclusion, it can be seen that the massive population growth in Seoul in the last thirty years has resulted in a number of negative factors. As the population has grown, the number of cars on the road has increased proportionately. The burden on the public transportation system is leading to longer delays in travel time which can then lead to rising stress levels. In addition, the growing pollution rate is a major concern for Seoul's inhabitants. Finally, with a greater demand in housing, prices are soaring across the city.

Activity 2

Look at the following thesis statements and details in the body. Paraphrase the thesis statement and add summary points.

Early life was not easy for the hopeful young soccer star, and yet, through the desperation and the difficulties, Edison Arantes do Nascimento rose to the top to become the greatest soccer player of all, Pelé.

B1: Living in poverty

B2: Hard work and dedication to soccer

B3: Becoming the best player in the world and winning the World Cup

_____

_____

_____

_____

_____

_____

English is a key that unlocks many opportunities, and for this reason, learning English is an important goal for most Korean students.

B1: Many prestigious universities in Korea use English as the language of instruction and teaching.

B2: Many companies in Korea now require employees to have a strong English ability.

B3: English allows students to travel with confidence and communicate with people in other countries.

_____

_____

_____

_____

_____

_____

_____

Conclude Memorably

Just as a hook helps to engage the readers by capturing their attention, the final sentences in the concluding paragraph can leave the reader with an interesting thought on the topic.

1. Make a prediction: What do you think will happen in the future?

> Tuition fees at Korean universities have been rising while at the same time, financial aid for students has been declining. **If this trend continues, fewer and fewer families will be able to send their children to university.**

2. Recommend an action to be followed (call to action): Making a final statement that advises an action to be taken can leave the reader with a strong impression with the reader. This is commonly used in persuasive writing.

> The cost of attending university in Korea has been increasing. Students are finding the financial strain to be too much with many dropping out of school. It is clear that the Korean system of higher education is in trouble. **To reverse this trend, students must demand that the government increase its financial support for universities and improve financial aid programs.**

3. End with a warning: What are the consequences of not taking action?

> With costs rising and financial aid declining, Korean university students are now facing a crisis with many dropping out or going to other countries to study. If Korea is to prosper in the future, the brightest young minds cannot be lost. **Without a change to the current system, Korea will not maintain its current position as a major economic power in Asia.**

4. Ask a provocative question: Engaging the reader by posing an interesting question is a great way to make a strong final impression.

> As people live much longer through the advancement of technology and better nutrition, the issues regarding adequate medical care becomes increasingly important. This is a situation that affects everyone and is an issue that people cannot ignore any longer. Society must approach this issue with great care and consideration. **What will the aging population do?**

5. Use a final quotation: Like an opening quote in a hook, a final quotation that ties in with the main idea is also a good method for creating a strong ending.

> With costs rising and financial aid declining, Korean university students are now facing a crisis. If Korea is to prosper in the future, Koreans cannot let their brightest young minds be lost. **As Kim, Sang Jun argued in his book,** *The Future Starts Now*, **"A nation's economic wealth will increase through an educated public"** (Kim 121). It is therefore imperative that students be given a "fair–go" so that they may build a better Korea.

Activity 3

In the following examples, the writer has restated the thesis statement and summarized the main point. Now add a memorable conclusion.

> Citizens of large cities have more choices with regard to entertainment and culture. In addition, it is easier to get a job, and the transportation is also more convenient. It is clear that living in a large city is better.
>
> _____
> _____
> _____
> _____
> _____
>
> In conclusion, the massive population growth in Seoul in the last thirty years has resulted in a number of negative factors. As the population has grown, the number of cars on the road has increased proportionately. The burden on the public transportation system is leading to longer delays in travel time, which can then lead to rising stress levels. In addition, increasing pollution is choking the city and is a major concern for Seoul's inhabitants. Finally, with a greater demand in housing, prices are soaring across the city.
>
> _____
> _____
> _____
> _____
> _____

For many Korean students, learning English is vital in opening the door to opportunity. Having a strong English language background can make university life easier and can help students to gain access to the best jobs after they graduate. In addition, it can also make travel easier and more enjoyable.

_____

_____

_____

_____

_____

What to Avoid in Your Conclusion

Never apologize or make a personal comment to the reader.

Example:

With costs rising and financial aid declining, Korean university students are now facing a crisis. If Korea is to prosper in the future, it is important to avoid losing the brightest young minds. **Sorry for my bad English. I tried my best ㅠㅠ.**

The conclusion is not the place to bring up new ideas.

Example:

With costs rising and financial aid declining, Korean university students are now facing a crisis. If Korea is to prosper in the future, we cannot let our brightest young minds be lost. **Korean universities also need to help students more by providing better research and study facilities.**

Do not finish with a sentimental or emotional statement.

Example:

As people live longer because of science and better nutrition, there will be greater problems in the future with an aging population. This is a situation that affects everyone and society cannot ignore it any longer. **I hope in the future that all the elderly people in the world can live happy lives.**

Activity 4

Read the three body paragraphs, and then add an introductory and concluding paragraph.

_____

_____

_____

_____

_____

_____

First, daily homework is important because it can help students to reinforce lecture notes. It is often difficult for students to understand everything in a lecture. Students are often tired, and it can be difficult to understand teachers. Therefore, homework is an important tool to reinforce classroom content. If students do not understand the content of the lectures during class time, it is easy for them to fall behind. To ensure that students keep up with the content of a lecture, doing homework is important.

While doing homework is important for reinforcing in-class learning, homework can also expose students to different ideas by giving them extra information not covered in class. At university, it is important for students to broaden their knowledge, but this is not always possible during class time. Due to time constraints, teachers cannot always cover everything about a topic. Therefore, in order to provide students with new ideas on a topic, teachers can give homework to their students.

Another strong argument for the necessity of homework is that it gives students the opportunity to share their own ideas. During university lectures, students do not always have the chance to voice their own opinions. In many lectures, students are simply passive learners only taking in the information given to them from the professors. By doing homework however, students can have a chance to apply classroom content and provide answers to questions. In this sense, homework can give students the opportunity to put forward their own ideas, which can enhance learning.

_____

_____

_____

_____

_____

Styles of Writing

While there are very general levels of writing complexity (sentences, paragraphs, reports), there are also specific styles or genres of writing that are used in different contexts. After learning the basics of sentences, paragraphs, and reports, this section will help writers to refine their skills, and tailor their writing to particular situations. Subsections of this chapter cover styles of writing, give examples, and help learners to understand how to improve their writing through various activities.

This section covers:

- Definition Writing
- Descriptive Writing
- Classification Writing
- Compare and Contrast Writing
- Cause and Effect Writing
- Persuasive Writing
- Reports
- Business Reports
- Social Science Reports

Definition Writing

1

The foundation of all types of academic writing is clearly defined terms. Words from other languages, cultural concepts, and new words often have to be clearly explained to help the audience understand what they are reading. In addition, the meaning of words can evolve over time, and technical language can be difficult to understand for people new to or outside of a discipline, so writers need to make sure that their readers understand the terminology they are using. Even in the work world, people need to be able to clearly explain and communicate products, concepts, and policies to clients and fellow employees alike.

Definitions are sometimes explored and communicated in-depth through entire paragraphs, and sometimes they are brief explanations encompassed in a few words. Thus, definition writing is essential for every subject and area of work, and students need to precisely and clearly explain the terms they are using.

In this section you will:

- Study how to briefly define terms
- Write brief definitions of academic terms
- Analyze definition paragraphs that provide in-depth examples of the defined term
- Develop, organize, and write a definition paragraph

What is Academic Vocabulary?

Academic vocabulary tends to be more formal and objective than conversational English. Students need to be familiar with these words to be successful at reading and writing at the university level. There are many lists of high-frequency words already compiled online.

Signpost Please see Victoria University of Wellington's "Academic Word List" for commonly used academic vocabulary.

https://www.wgtn.ac.nz/lals/resources/academicwordlist

Students also need to know how to succinctly define these words.

Example: In academia, *authority* refers to people or sources which are recognized as influential because of extensive or specialized knowledge.

Signpost Please see the section on italics and quotation marks on page 210 and simple adjective clauses on page 188 for more practice in how to properly incorporate academic writing into assignments.

Activity 1

On a separate piece of paper, write one sentence definitions for the following academic terms using the model above. If you do not know what the word means, look it up in the dictionary. However, when you write your own sentence, make sure you use your own words to describe the term.

Traditional	Compensation	Hypothesis
Diversity	Commodity	Empirical
Perspective	Currency	Variables

What Is a Definition Paragraph?

While some academic or discipline-specific terms are briefly defined, others require more elaboration in definition paragraphs. In this case, definitions are illustrated with major and minor details to give readers explicit examples of what the term means.

Write Right

"Plagiarism" is an academic term that means inappropriately using other material in one's own work. First, some writers have a problem with source plagiarism. When writers use research or quotes from other sources, they need to state where the information comes from in an in-text citation and include a reference page at the end of their work. However, if they do not fully or correctly acknowledge the sources they used, this can lead readers to mistakenly believe the research and ideas are the authors' own. Secondly, writers can also commit partial plagiarism. Sometimes this happens when writers too closely follow the original words and sentence structure instead of properly paraphrasing or summarizing the material they used. In other cases, writers piece together small parts of various people's work. In both situations, authors have done some work to find the information, but they have not done enough to phrase ideas in their own words or analyse concepts. Finally, some writers are guilty of direct plagiarism. In this case, they take a whole piece of writing from a print or digital source without any kind of attribution. This kind of plagiarism means that writers have not done any of the writing by themselves and are fully passing off others' work as their own. Thus, writers should be very careful to avoid plagiarism when they write, so they do not get in trouble for accidently or intentionally plagiarising.

Activity 2

1. Circle the topic.

2. Underline the controlling idea.

In a definition paragraph, the topic sentence is a definition of the term. Supporting details need to show examples of the definition.

3. Fill in the following supporting details chart. Do the supporting details match the definition in the topic sentence?

	Major Details	**Minor Details**
1.		
2.		
3.		

Activity 3

Step 1: With your partner, brainstorm a list of terms that are common in your major but might need to be explained to someone outside of your discipline.

Step 2: Pick one term and write your own succinct definition for the word using a simple adjective clause. This will become your topic sentence.

_____

_____

Step 3: Brainstorm three examples that illustrate your definition. Ensure that your examples match your topic sentence and show various examples of the term you are defining or various ways it is used.

	Major Details	**Minor Details**
1.		
2.		
3.		

Step 4: Combine the topic sentence and supporting sentences into a properly-formatted paragraph and add a concluding sentence. Then, exchange your paragraph with another group. After they have read your paragraph, ask them to write another example of your term to see if they have understood its meaning.

_____

_____

_____

_____

_____

_____

_____

_____

_____

_____

_____

_____

Defining Words from Other Languages

Definitions are also important when describing cultural concepts or words from another language. While these words may not have an easy English translation, they are often understandable concepts that can easily be conveyed to readers from another cultural or linguistic background if appropriate examples are given.

To ensure a well-organized paragraph that flows well, many writers use major details that are all connected. For example, one term might be connected to three different types of people, places, companies, or news stories, while another term could be explained by writing about three situations in which the term might be used.

Activity 4

Look at the following topic sentence, which is also a definition. With a partner, brainstorm your examples illustrating the definition. Then look at the full paragraph on the next page to compare your ideas with the paragraph's supporting details.

Topic Sentence: *Schadenfreude* is a German word which refers to the joy people feel when they observe others' suffering.

	Major Details (Brainstormed Examples)	Major Details (Paragraph Examples)	Minor Details (Brainstormed Examples)	Minor Details (Paragraph Examples)
1.				
2.				
3.				

Schadenfreude: Wiping Tears with Joy

Schadenfreude is a German word which refers to the joy people feel when they observe others' suffering. First, schadenfreude is regularly felt between classmates. Students often get annoyed when their parents berate them for not getting high marks like the best student. However, if the top student fails to do well on the university entrance exam, other students often take great pleasure in the "best" student's poor performance. Similarly, sports fans rejoice when a top ranked team or their arch nemesis loses in competition. Brazil's spectacular 7-1 loss to Germany in the 2014 FIFA World Cup resulted in schadenfreude among German football enthusiasts who are used to seeing Brazil dominate in competition. Furthermore, people regularly feel schadenfreude when it comes to politicians. Voters who back the winning party in an election feel a sense of glee as they watch the losing party's candidate give a concession speech on election night. Thus, even though English does not have a direct translation for schadenfreude, when it comes classmates, sports opponents, and political figures, most people have experienced feeling enjoyment when they see others' troubles.

Activity 5

English does not have a direct translation for the any of the following Korean terms, but readers can still understand the concept of each word with the help of a definition and examples. Choose one of the words, and write a definition paragraph based on the *schadenfreude* paragraph model. Make sure your supporting details focus on clear examples to help your readers understand how to use the term instead of giving extensive linguistic background about the term's etymology.

정	눈치	체면	막장	사차원
한	효	애교	갑질	흙수저

2 Descriptive Writing

Unlike other forms of writing found later in this section, descriptive writing is not a way to structure your writing. Instead, it is a style of writing that invokes the senses or provides more detail using adjectives, adverbs, and more precise vocabulary to paint a picture for your reader. In other words, writers do not tell their readers what something is; they show what they want to convey through their descriptions.

Descriptive writing is not usually used for formal academic writing. It is more often used in advertising and marketing campaigns to promote new or improved products, in tourism to attract tourists, and in narrative writing to build characters, setting, and atmosphere.

In this section you will:

- Examine two different descriptive paragraphs
- Learn to identify and build atmosphere through descriptive words
- Learn about the differences between connotation and denotation
- Identify the connotation and denotation of various words
- Practice describing objects using precise vocabulary
- Brainstorm for descriptive writing
- Write your own assignments using the tools you have developed in this section

Answer the following questions about places you have been.

1. Think about the best place you have visited. What words would you use to describe this place?

2. What was is the worst place you have visited? What words would you use to describe this place?

Descriptive Paragraph Example 1

Heaven on Earth

Paradise Beach is a fabulous place for a holiday. This private, secluded beach is an ideal place to spend a relaxing and peaceful vacation. For instance, this pristine area features kilometers of silky sand that is soft to lie on and warm on the toes. Stretching in front on the beach are the calm waters of the Pacific Ocean. Visitors relaxing on the beach enjoy the fragrant sea breeze while watching the waves gently lap and roll onto the sand. Later, when the sun rises high in the endless sky devoid of clouds, the ocean's clear waters become even more inviting and refreshing. Thus, as a vacation destination, no other beach can compare to this tranquil heavenly spot.

Descriptive Paragraph Example 2

Paradise Is Hell

Paradise Beach is a wretched place to take a vacation. Because of its isolation from other tourist areas and the dreadful natural surroundings, Paradise Beach is a desolate place. The sand is gritty and rough on sensitive toes, and the beach is littered with garbage from the dark waters of the Pacific Ocean. Even when a spot devoid of waste is found on the beach, holidaymakers rarely stay as the sweltering heat scorches the sand and makes it unbearable to relax. However, the menacing ocean brings no relief for overheated vacationers as the violent, crashing waves are enough to terrify even the most advanced swimmers. In addition, the putrid sea breeze warns of water polluted by waste, and the dull grey sky is menacing. Therefore, if travelers want a spot to experience heaven on Earth, Paradise Beach is the last place they should go for a blissful vacation.

Activity 2

Highlight the descriptive words used in the example paragraphs. Then fill in the following chart to see the differences in the words used to describe various nouns in the passages.

Noun	Paragraph 1	Paragraph 2
Beach/Area		
Sand		
Ocean/Waves		
Sea breeze		
Sky/Sun		

Activity 3

Choose another noun that you would find at a beach, and write it in the empty section of the chart above. Then think of several words you could use to describe the noun for both paragraphs. Afterward, write your own additional sentence in your notebook for each of these paragraphs by incorporating these descriptive words.

Connotation and Denotation

"Denotation" means the dictionary definition of a word while "connotation" refers to the emotional meaning; therefore, while two words have the same meaning, they do not always invoke the same feeling.

The government **brainwashed** its citizens into agreeing to the new law.
The government **persuaded** its citizens to agree with the new law.

Both words mean "finding a way to get another person to agree with an opinion;" however, "brainwashed" has a very negative connotation because it sounds irrational while "persuaded" means that people have become convinced through thoughtful arguments.

Activity 4

Complete the following passage by filling in your own words. Afterward, share your story with your classmates and see if there are any differences in your stories based on the words you chose.

The _____ house with _____ windows and a _____ door was located on the corner of the _____ street. It was surrounded by _____ trees, _____ flowers, and a _____ gate. The house looked like it should be in a _____ movie. From time to time, people would walk by the house and remark at how _____ it looked. Although many people wanted to live there, in the end they decided against buying the property because it was _____.

Activity 5

Categorize the following words as negative or positive.

1. pushy, aggressive, assertive
2. curious, nosy, prying, inquisitive
3. lazy, leisurely, relaxing, slothful
4. youthful, immature, childish
5. unique, strange, weird, exceptional, distinctive, extraordinary
6. carefree, irresponsible, negligent, lax
7. rude, frank, honest, straightforward, candid, imprudent

Positive	Negative
1.	
2.	
3.	
4.	
5.	
6.	
7.	

Activity 6

Choose one of the following topics and brainstorm common nouns for that topic in the chart below. Afterwards, think about some positive and negative ways to describe each noun. It may help you to think about the following categories of words: sight, taste, sound, touch, smell, or characteristics.

1. A person you know

2. A historical person

3. The person sitting across from you on a blind date

4. A vacation destination (real or imagined)

5. A new restaurant

6. An apartment for sale

7. A pet

8. A newly discovered animal

9. A new electronic product

10. A new car

Noun	Positive	Negative

Activity 7

After brainstorming both positive and negative words for your topic, write two different paragraphs using these words. Then have your partner read your paragraphs, and highlight the words that convey positive or negative meaning.

Signpost See page 186 for more information on the order of adjectives. In general, you should not write more than three adjectives and a determiner before one noun.

Classification Writing

Classification writing is a way of organizing or sorting ideas or items into categories. In a classification paragraph or essay, the writer describes and develops ideas by sorting the contents into groups or classes. Classification is often used by scientists to show the relationship between living organisms. Dance or physical education students may need to use classification as a way to describe and analyze types of dance or sport. Classification is also utilized by businesses and individuals as a means of exploring market research or products. Classification writing can be used with almost any subject.

In this section you will:

- Examine a model classification paragraph and essay
- Analyze the organization of a classification essay
- Write a classification paragraph or essay

Activity 1

Complete the following questions and then read the essay.

1. Have you ever watched a television program or movie featuring a character that was a monster or mythical creature?
   Check the ones you have seen.

   _____ zombies   _____ ghosts   _____ vampires   _____ dragons

   _____ aliens   _____ werewolves   _____ demons   _____ sea monsters

   Other _____

2. If you were confronted by a vampire, zombie, or werewolf, what would you do?

Understanding the Threat

Monstrous and evil figures have existed in legend for thousands of years, and in the last century with the arrival of film and television the concept of the monster has been pushed further into the forefront of popular culture. In recent times a more romantic view of monsters and mythological figures has been portrayed. In the popular novel and movie *Twilight*, characters like Edward Cullen and Jacob Black are not seen as terrifying or gruesome but instead as sexy and charming. In the animation series *Shrek*, the large green ogre is a peaceful hero who falls in love with a princess. In reality, nothing could be further from the truth. Monsters are not cute, sexy, or cool, and they should be feared at all times. A healthy knowledge of the characteristics of certain monsters and mythological figures is not only advisable, but also necessary if people wish to live a long life.

Perhaps the most well-known and documented mythological being is the vampire. In her book *The Vampire as Numinous Experience*, author Beth E. McDonald describes vampires as being "undead creatures resembling living humans who feed on the living by drinking the victim's blood" (21). The modern day vampire is depicted as healthy on the surface, able to talk and pass as human, and usually possessing of extraordinary or supernatural powers. Vampires create others like them when they bite their victim. A common belief regarding transformation is that when a vampire bites or feeds on a human, a retrovirus in the saliva or blood transforms the human into a vampire. Vampires usually react negatively to religious objects and also folk remedies such as garlic, wild rose, and mountain ash. It is also widely believed that weapons of silver, exposure to direct sunlight, and impaling a vampire through the heart with a wooden stake will kill them. Therefore, vampires are one the most fearsome of all mythological figures, and preparation is vital if one wishes to retain the upper hand.

Another monster that has been popularized in film and television is the zombie. While vampires are often described as "the undead," zombies are regarded as "the living dead." Kyle William Bishop in his book *American Gothic Zombie* describes the zombie as a corpse raised from the dead with pale skin, a vacant stare, and a decomposing body (110). Although zombies may walk upright and appear human from a distance, they are essentially dead and have no developed brain functions. As a result, they "cannot process information, learn from their mistakes, act in their own self-interests, or even speak. Instead zombies act on instinct and drive alone" (110). Similar to the vampire, the zombie is able to transform its victim by biting and infecting the victim. In popular film and television, zombiism appears to be viral with the victim first dying from a zombie attack before rising from the dead. However, unlike their undead counterpart the vampire, zombies cannot be injured or destroyed by religious symbols or plants. A zombie can be beaten, stabbed, torn limb from limb, or shot but the body will still continue on its relentless pursuit of human flesh if the brain is still intact. Thus, the only sure way to kill a zombie is to destroy its already rotting brain.

Another mythological creature that strikes fear into the heart and mind is the werewolf. The werewolf, also known as a lycanthrope, is a beast able to change between human and wolf form. Cryptozoologist Peter Velps describes werewolves as large wolf-like creatures with superhuman strength and increased senses (27). The mythology surrounding the werewolf reveals there are two ways of becoming a werewolf. First, lycanthropy is a hereditary condition, so a child can be born a werewolf. Second, a person can be turned into a werewolf if they are bitten by one. Like the zombie, werewolves are thought not to be affected by religious symbols, but they can be repelled by the herbs wolfsbane and mountain ash. It is thought that the only way to kill a werewolf is with weapons of silver like a silver sword or a silver bullet. Once a suspected werewolf is killed, the wolf will transform into human form and die. Therefore, if the creature killed does not transform back into human form, run. The werewolf is still out there.

Monsters and evil creatures have been around for centuries. While most people dismiss the notion of the existence of monsters, there are still some believers. Film goers may have fallen in love with Edward Cullen, but it should always be remembered that a vampire is an extremely dangerous adversary and should never be underestimated. In the unlikely event of a zombie apocalypse, stay quiet and out of sight. Do not assume that friends and family members are what they seem. Werewolves are brutally strong and fast, so trying to escape on foot is useless. Plant some wolfsbane in apartment gardens and stay inside when there is a full moon. Frank Herbert the acclaimed science fiction author said, "The beginning of knowledge is the discovery of something we do not understand (1)." In order to be fully prepared for the unexplained, learn about it first. It might be the difference between life and death.

Activity 2

Some people believe that monsters are not just real, but may be actually living in our communities. If a classmate, friend, or family member were a type of monster, who would it be and what type? Why do you suspect this? Discuss with a partner.

Organization of a Classification Essay

Once a topic has been chosen, the organization of the essay is fairly easy. If the writer wishes to examine three places to visit in France, the essay will have three body paragraphs. Similarly, if the writer decides to look at four main features on a DSLR camera, the body will be comprised of four body paragraphs.

Parallel Paragraph Structure

In a classification essay, each body paragraph should contain the same supporting details. In an essay on places to visit in France, if the writer examines things to see, accommodation, and places to eat in the city of Paris, then the same three features should be used when writing about the other two places in France.

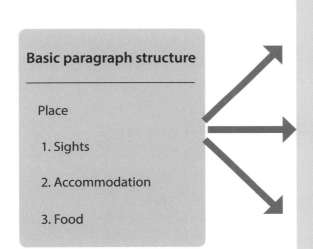

Basic paragraph structure

Place

1. Sights

2. Accommodation

3. Food

1. Body Paragraph 1: Paris
   a. Supporting detail 1: Things to see
   b. Supporting detail 2: Accommodation
   c. Supporting detail 3: Places to eat

2. Body Paragraph 2: French Riviera
   a. Supporting detail 1: Things to see
   b. Supporting detail 2: Accommodation
   c. Supporting detail 3: Places to eat

3. Body Paragraph 1: Provence
   a. Supporting detail 1: Things to see
   b. Supporting detail 2: Accommodation
   c. Supporting detail3: Places to eat

Activity 3

Go back to the essay "Understanding the Threat." Does the body have parallel structure? What are the three features examined in the body paragraph?

a. Supporting detail 1: _____

b. Supporting detail 2: _____

c. Supporting detail 3: _____

Activity 4

Choose one of the following topics and create a body outline for a classification essay.

1. Computer games
2. The different coffee shops in Hyehwa
3. Singers/bands
4. University majors

Body Paragraph 1: _____

   a. Supporting detail _____

      _____

   b. Supporting detail _____

      _____

   c. Supporting detail _____

      _____

Body Paragraph 2: _____

   a. Supporting detail _____

      _____

   b. Supporting detail _____

      _____

   c. Supporting details _____

      _____

Body Paragraph 3: _____

   a. Supporting detail _____

      _____

   b. Supporting detail _____

      _____

   c. Supporting detail _____

      _____

Activity 5

Using the information from your body outline in Activity 4, write a full essay with introduction and conclusion in your notebook.

Compare and Contrast Writing

Compare and contrast writing takes two or more topics and examines their similarities, differences, or similarities and differences. Unlike persuasive writing, compare and contrast writing does not make a judgement or take a particular stance on how one topic is better or worse than the other. Rather, this type of writing looks at the topics objectively. However, even though you will be comparing or contrasting two or more different topics, you need to make sure that you still have one thesis statement. In addition, you should also give an approximately equal amount of space to both topics to ensure a balanced assignment.

Compare and contrast writing is often used in academic writing to objectively examine multiple topics or options. For example, students might look at two dynasties in a history class, different products in a business paper, or more than one styles of dance in a performing arts program. Nevertheless, employees may also use compare and contrast writing in a non-academic context in order to compare two different financial packages available at a bank or credit card company, explore two travel options for a tourist agency, or various course choices at a university.

In this section you will:

- Learn different kinds of compare and contrast structure
- Examine a compare and contrast essay
- Learn to identify good and bad topic combinations
- Practice Venn Diagram and T-Chart brainstorming
- Use compare and contrast connecting words
- Write your own compare and contrast assignment using the skills learned in this section

Activity 1

Answer the following questions about holidays.

1. What is your favorite holiday? What do you like most about this holiday?

2. How do you think traditional holidays like Chuseok and Seollal will change in fifty years?

Thanksgiving and Chuseok: Unique Festivals for Unique Cultures

Many cultures around the world hold festivals or celebrate special days devoted to being thankful for newly harvested food. In the United States of America, Thanksgiving, which is held on the 4th Thursday in November, is one of the most important holidays. Likewise, Koreans have a traditional festival held on the 15th day of the 8th lunar month called Chuseok. Both of these holidays occur in autumn, and Americans and Koreans eat special dishes comprised of local produce with their family members. However, despite these similarities, differences in the origin, focus, and traditional activities make Thanksgiving and Chuseok very distinct holidays.

While both Thanksgiving and Chuseok are holidays that date back several centuries, their origins are very different from each other. Previous to European explorers and colonists encountering the North American continent, many Europeans and Native Americans had autumn harvest festivals. Evidence suggests that Spanish explorers held a special holiday as early as the mid-sixteenth century, but the current holiday's origin is traced back to British settlers in Plymouth, celebrating a particularly good harvest in 1621 (Smith 4). On the other hand, Chuseok is a more ancient holiday originating in the Shilla Dynasty. It probably began as a celebration after a weaving competition, but it may have also been part of a celebration held after an important win over the Balhae Kingdom. Only later did this festival take on a stronger agricultural meaning related to the harvest and new moon. Therefore, while both Thanksgiving and Chuseok are very old festivals, they have very different origins and histories.

In addition to a harvest festival, today, both Americans and Koreans give thanks and show gratitude during their special holidays, but the focus of these feelings is different. Because Americans usually gather with their family members during the holiday, they often spend time reflecting on the importance of family and community. However, the present-day Thanksgiving holiday has also expanded to being thankful for many other parts of life, including health, employment, and new opportunities. In contrast, because of strong shaman and Confucian traditions in Korea, Chuseok has become not only a time to spend with living family members, but also a time to honor and reflect on ancestors. Thus, while Americans reflect on the first Thanksgiving celebrations, most of their attention is on the present and their current blessings. In contrast, Koreans are more concerned with honoring the ancestors who made this life possible.

Finally, the differences between the origin and focus of Thanksgiving and Chuseok mean that the activities that Americans and Koreans participate in during their holidays are also different, with the exception of meeting with family members and eating elaborate meals. In the United States, students often participate in plays idealizing early Thanksgiving celebrations between Native Americans and Europeans. In addition, on the actual holiday, families watch parades or football games together in an effort to spend time with their loved ones. However, because honoring the dead is an important part of Chuseok, many Koreans participate in *charye*, which is an ancestral memorial ritual. Koreans also visit family burial plots to clean graves. After these duties are completed, they may watch archery or Korean wrestling competitions called *ssireum*, which date back to the Shilla Dynasty. In this way, both Americans and Koreans spend the holiday with their family members, but their activities reflect their different cultures.

In conclusion, Thanksgiving and Chuseok are often anticipated holidays because Americans and Koreans can spend time with their families while enjoying good seasonal food. However, despite these similarities, and the fact that Chuseok is often translated into English as "Korean Thanksgiving," the two holidays have many differences. The different origins and focuses of these festivals have impacted the kinds of activities that have become customary. These differences which make the holidays unique festivals that both Americans and Koreans should learn about to understand the distinctiveness of American and Korean culture.

Activity 2

Answer the following questions about the essay you have just read.

1. Does this essay focus more on the similarities or the differences between the two holidays?

2. Make a list of the similarities and differences between two other holidays.

Structure

There are three basic structures found in compare and contrast writing: focus on the similarities, focus on the differences, and focus on the similarities and differences. The following structural examples are based on comparing and contrasting North American and Korean Christmas.

Focus on the Similarities

Paragraph	Topic	Korean and North American Information
Body Paragraph 1	Food	Eaten with loved ones, special desserts
Body Paragraph 2	Symbols	Christmas tree, red and green, lights
Body Paragraph 3	Santa	Santa – large man who wears red, beard, delivers gifts
	Myth	

Focus on the Differences

Paragraph	Topic	Korean Information	North American Information
Body Paragraph 1	Food	Who: eaten with romantic partner or friends at a restaurant What: pizza, steak, wine, purchased Christmas cake	Who: eaten with family at home What: homemade turkey, ham, or goose, Christmas cookies, traditional dried fruit cake
Body Paragraph 2	Decorations	Mostly public: shopping areas, major streets, city areas Home: perhaps a small tree	Equally public and private: elaborate indoor and outdoor displays in homes, businesses, and public places
Body Paragraph 3	Santa Myth	1 reindeer (Rudolph), unknown home, family, and life	Several (perhaps 9) reindeer, Santa lives at the North Pole with his wife (Mrs. Claus) and elves (who make the toys)

Focus on the Similarities and Differences

Paragraph	Topic	Similarities	Differences
Body Paragraph 1	Food	Eaten with loved ones, special desserts	Korea: romantic partner/friends at restaurant eating pizza, steak, wine North America: family at home, homemade turkey, ham, or goose, Christmas cookies, traditional fruit cake
Body Paragraph 2	Decorations	Christmas tree, red and green, lights	Korea: mostly public, perhaps a small tree at home North America: elaborate indoor and outdoor displays in homes, businesses, and public areas
Body Paragraph 3	Santa Myth	Santa – large man who wears red, beard, delivers gifts	Korea: 1 reindeer, Santa's life unknown North America: 9 reindeer, North Pole, wife, helpers

Topic Selection

When choosing your topics for a compare and contrast assignment, you need to make sure that the topics are neither too similar nor too different. For instance, hamburgers and cheeseburgers are too similar to each other with the exception of a slice of cheese. In contrast, while ice cream and Siberia are both cold, the similarities end there. While deciding what you are going to write about, you should find two topics that are part of the same category with enough differences to make your paper interesting.

Activity 3

Look at the following topics and mark if they are too similar (S), too different (D), or good topics for a compare and contrast essay (G).

1. *Kimbap* vs. sandwiches
2. Japan vs. Japan Airlines (JAL)
3. Scuba diving vs. space walking
4. Caffé latte vs. Americano
5. Action movie vs. Korean drama

6. Seollal vs. Solar New Year's Day
7. Turtles vs. snails
8. *Gochujang* vs. *jjimjilbang*
9. Seoul vs. Gyeongju
10. Vampires vs. witches

Venn Diagram Brainstorming

There are two ways to brainstorm for compare and contrast assignments. The first way is a Venn diagram, which is a visual way to show the similarities and differences between two topics. The following Venn Diagram shows the similarities and differences between Thanksgiving in the United States and Chuseok in South Korea.

4th Tuesday in November (solar calendar – 1 day)

Safe travels to North America, thankful for current blessings

Turkey, stuffing, mashed potatoes, cranberry sauce, pumpkin/ sweet potato pie

Watching parades and football games

Autumn

Harvest festival
Family holiday

Seasonal food

Family dinner

15th day of the 8th month (lunar calendar – 3 days)

Shilla Dynasty-weaving festival + victory over Balhae, Confucianism

Bulgogi, japchae, jeon, songpyeon, fruit, *toranguk*

Charye, traditional sports (*ssireum*, archery)

T-Chart Brainstorming

The second way to brainstorm for a compare and contrast assignment is a T-chart. This method works better for longer and more complicated assignments because there is more space available to develop each point. In this type of brainstorming, write the category on the left side and brainstorm the similarities and differences for each topic in the other columns. To differentiate between similarities and differences, use different colors of highlighters or underline the points that are different.

Category	The United States: Thanksgiving	Korea: Chuseok
When	• 4th Thursday in November • Solar calendar • Public holiday: One day	• 15th day of the 8th month • Lunar calendar • Public holiday: Three-five days
Origin	• Spanish 16th century/British 17th century • European and Native American harvest festivals • Good harvest/safe travels to North America	• Shilla Dynasty • A feast after a weaving contest • Victory over Balhae kingdom
Current Focus	• Family holiday • Harvest festival • Being thankful for present blessings	• Family holiday • Harvest festival • Ancestral memorial rituals
Food	• Turkey • Stuffing, mashed potatoes, sweet potatoes, squash • Pumpkin or sweet potato pie	• *Bulgogi* • *Japchae, jeon, toranguk* • *Songpyeon*, fruit
Activities	• Family dinner • Parades • Football games	• Family dinner • *Charye* and cleaning ancestors' graves • Traditional sports: *ssireum*, archery, tug of war

Compare and Contrast Connecting Words

Throughout your compare and contrast assignment, you should use connecting words to connect ideas and to make smooth transitions between different sections. The following are examples of both types of words.

Compare (Similarities)

likewise	similarly	furthermore	in addition	additionally
as	in the same way	also	too	moreover

Contrast (Differences)

yet	however	alternatively	conversely	although
in contrast	on the other hand	on the contrary	but	nevertheless

Activity 4

Take one of the good topic combinations in Activity 3, and brainstorm the similarities and differences in your notebook using a Venn diagram.

Activity 5

Use the ideas you brainstormed in Activity 4, and link them with connecting words to make full sentences.

Signpost See pages 14, 15, and 36 for more information on connecting words. Some of the connecting words given above are coordinating conjunctions while others are subordinating conjunction words or transitions. Make sure you understand the differences between these kinds of words before you make your own sentences.

Activity 6

Use the sentences you made in Activity 5 to write a well-organized paragraph by adding a topic sentence and concluding sentence.

5 Cause and Effect Writing

Cause and effect writing shows the relationship between one idea or event and another, and thus, it is a common style found in academic assignments, essays, and reports.

In business classes, students may be required to examine the negative effects of high staff turnover or describe the reasons for low product sales. Engineering students may need to investigate the failings of a weight-bearing structure in a collapsed building or the effects of soil erosion. Students of history will often be asked to examine the causes and effects of historical events.

Cause and effect writing is favored by many teachers and professors because it requires the students to demonstrate critical thinking skills and analyze how events are related and connected to each other.

In this section you will:

- examine a model cause and effect essay
- analyze the different methods and organizational patterns of cause and effect writing
- examine how cause and effect connectors are used to show a relationship
- write a cause and effect essay.

Activity 1

Answer the following questions about Cheonggyecheon.

1. Have you ever visited Cheonggyecheon? What are Cheonggyecheon's features?

2. What do you think are some of the advantages or disadvantages of having a stream or river flowing through the center of a city?

The Restoration of Cheonggyecheon

On July 1st, 2003, an ambitious plan led by the then mayor of Seoul, Lee, Myung Bak, began to restore the historic 600-year-old Cheonggyecheon stream that had been covered by road and expressway for over 30 years. The project was to take over two years and cost over 350 billion won, and it would eventually transform and revitalize the old central business district in Gangbuk, Seoul. When completed on September 30th, 2005, a green pathway along a 5.86 kilometer section of the 10.92 kilometer stream was unveiled that would become one of the most popular tourist attractions in Seoul. Dr. K.Y. Hwang described Cheonggyecheon as a symbol of the transformation of Seoul into a world class city (89). There have been a number of positive effects resulting from the restoration of Cheonggycheon, with the project becoming a vehicle for environmental change, economic revitalization, and cultural renaissance.

One of the most noticeable and immediate effects of the Cheonggyecheon restoration project was the improvement in environmental quality in the Gangbuk central business district (CBD). As a result of the removal of the elevated highway that stood above the historic waterway and the reorganization of the public transport system, a dramatic reduction in the amount of traffic entering downtown ensued. Consequently, air quality improved drastically. In addition to a decrease in air pollution, the reduction of vehicles helped to reduce the temperature in the downtown area. The removal of the existing elevated highway, in conjunction with the flow of water and air down the stream, resulted in a reduction in temperature in the CBD of around 10-13% (91). Environmental quality has also been enhanced by the creation of new natural habitats along the stream, thus many bird and insect species have returned. In addition, the introduction of various species of fish into the stream has also contributed to the re-establishment of Cheonggyecheon as a living space. As a consequence of the enhancement of atmospheric quality and the construction of green spaces, a new ecologically friendly environment has been created for citizens to enjoy.

In addition to the environmental transformation, the restoration of Cheonggyecheon has also helped to revitalize the CBD and stimulate economic development. During the last few decades, Seoul city has focused its efforts on developing the Gangnam area; as a consequence, the old CBD located in Gangbuk had contracted (85). One of the main objectives of the Cheonggyecheon restoration project was to initiate a balanced development between north and south Seoul, and the revitalization of the Cheonggyecheon area helped this considerably. The Cheonggyecheon project has been a catalyst for urban expansion and commercial success in the area resulting in the return of both international and national regional headquarters to the Gangbuk area around the Cheonggyecheon. For example, in early 2011 the 80 billion won Mirae Assets Center One Building was opened alongside the historic stream. There can be no doubt that the vitality of the Gangbuk CBD has been greatly enhanced by the restoration of Cheonggyecheon.

Finally, the restoration of Cheonggyecheon has resulted in the re-establishment of the culture and historical heritage in and around the Gangbuk area. According to Kim, Nam Joon, a professor in the Department of Landscape Architecture at Dankook University, "The restoration project of Cheonggyecheon is, not only a part of Seoul's urban planning, but a symbolic project to revive an important part of Korea's historical and natural heritage at the start of the twenty-first century" (81). Due to the restoration of historical objects like Gwangtonggyo Bridge, many of the cultural treasures hidden from the citizens of Seoul for decades have been uncovered again. To create a synergy between culture and tourism, the Seoul Foundation for the Arts and Culture has initiated a number of festivals, including the Cheonggyecheon Art Festival and the Seoul Lantern Festival, both held in the Cheonggyecheon area. As a consequence, the Gangbuk CBD is regaining its position in Seoul as the place to be. For over six centuries, Cheonggyecheon itself was a part of the culture and heritage of Seoul. Now, after three decades of being buried, it is once again in the spotlight and has led to a cultural renaissance in Seoul.

In conclusion, since its re-opening in September 2005, Cheonggyecheon has become a beneficial feature in the lives of Seoulites. The restoration of the historic waterway has helped to invigorate the local environment through the creation of a cooler, healthier CBD, and the re-creation of natural habitats has resulted in life returning to an area that had been choking on automobile exhaust for almost 30 years. Economic balance in Seoul has been restored as investors have returned to the old CBD; thus, the local economy has been revitalized. Most importantly, perhaps, Cheonggyecheon has provided a cultural green space and events venue for both Korean citizens and overseas tourists to enjoy. There is no doubt that Cheonggyecheon is once again an important asset to the citizens of Seoul. In the future it will continue to be loved and enjoyed by the people who use it, making it the veritable soul of the city.

Activity 2

Answer the following questions about the essay.

1. Does this essay state the effects from the restoration of Cheonggyecheon, the causes for the restoration of Cheonggyecheon, or both?

2. What are the three main effects of the restoration of Cheonggyecheon? For each body idea, find three supporting examples stated in the essay.

B1 _____

B2 _____

B3 _____

3. In your town or city, choose a historic, famous, or interesting place, and write down any effects it may have on the citizens and the town/city itself.

_____
_____
_____
_____
_____
_____

Organization of a Cause-Effect Essay

Once a topic has been given or chosen, the way the essay will be organized should be decided. A writer may wish to examine the causes, effects, or both.

Focus on Causes Method

Using this method, the writer will discuss the causes for an event or condition and develop and discuss each cause in each body paragraph. In the following example, the writer will discuss the factors that can cause heart disease to increase.

A person has a poor diet.	
A person smokes.	The risk of heart disease increases.
A person has a family history of high blood pressure.	

Focus on Effects Method

Using this method, the writer will discuss the effects of an event or condition and develop and discuss each effect in each body paragraph. In the following example, the writer will discuss the effects resulting from a poor diet.

	They may gain weight.
People have a poor diet.	They may suffer from fatigue.
	They may develop Type II diabetes.

Activity 3

Fill in the tables with appropriate information to complete the cause-effect relationship.

Ji Su goes to the library every day.	
Ji Su studies hard on the weekends.	
Ji Su takes extra classes.	

A country hosts the Olympic Games.	

Focus on Causes and Effects Method (Chain Organization)

Using this method, the writer will discuss both the causes and effects of an event or condition. The effect from the previous paragraph will then become the cause in the preceding paragraph. The causes and effects are therefore linked like a chain with each having an influence on the next. In the following example, the writer will discuss the links leading from a poor diet to an increase in the risk of heart disease.

How diet affects health

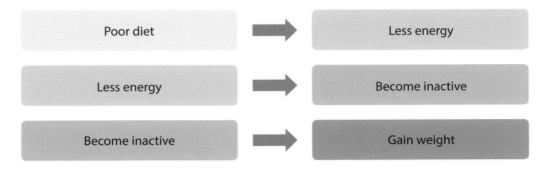

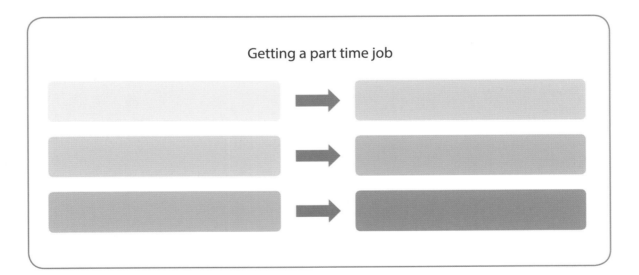

Getting a part time job

Signpost When developing ideas in a chain organization, the writer needs to be careful to avoid logical fallacies. See page 212-213.

Cause-Effect Organization

When developing the causes or effects in an essay, you can organize the body in two ways: order of importance and chronological (time) order.

1. Order of importance: This format is where ideas are arranged from the weakest to the strongest. In the essay on the restoration of Cheonggyecheon, the writer believes that the re-establishment of the cultural and historical heritage is the most important factor. A different writer, such as an economics or business major, may feel that the stimulation of the local economy is the most important and thereby the final effect to discuss.

2. Chronological order: This format is where ideas are arranged into a time order from what happened first to last. Cause-effect writing dealing with history is often arranged chronologically.

Cause-Effect Connecting Words

Just as connecting words are used in other types of writing, so too are they used to show or express the relationship between ideas.

Cause

Because Since As	the costs were high,	the project was canceled
As a result of As a consequence of Because of Due to	the high costs	

Effect

The costs were too high;	as a result, as a consequence, thus, therefore, consequently, hence,	the project was canceled

Activity 4

In the model essay, a number of connectors have been used to show the cause/effect relationship. Go back through the essay and highlight any cause/effect connectors.

Activity 5

Choose one of the three following topics, and create the body outline for an essay. What method of organization will you use?

| The growth of Seoul | The high divorce rate | Increased life expectancy |

1. Body Paragraph 1: _____

   a. Supporting detail 1: _____

   _____

   b. Supporting detail 2: _____

   _____

   c. Supporting detail 3: _____

   _____

2. Body Paragraph 2: _____

   a. Supporting detail 1: _____

   _____

   b. Supporting detail 2: _____

   _____

   c. Supporting detail 3: _____

   _____

3. Body Paragraph 3: _____

   a. Supporting detail 1: _____

   _____

   b. Supporting detail 2: _____

   _____

   c. Supporting detail 3: _____

   _____

Activity 6

Using what you have learned so far, write a cause and effect essay.

Persuasive Writing

Persuasive writing is writing in which writers give their opinion and the reasons for their opinion with the aim of convincing the reader to agree with them. The writer appeals to logic and evidence in order to make a strong case for their argument and addresses the questions or objections the reader may have. Good persuasive writing should include sufficient evidence, and this requires research on the part of the writer.

We are constantly exposed to persuasion through the media and through interactions with our friends. We are persuaded to buy products, watch shows and films, listen to music, read publications, and of course, believe certain opinions. Persuasive writing is one method of presenting a convincing message or argument to an audience of readers. You might want to persuade a prospective employer to invite you for an interview, or maybe you want to persuade people to avoid using a particular telephone service after your own bad experience. Maybe you are passionate about a current issue, and you wish to convince others to think in the same way.

Persuasive strategies also increase your awareness of the subtle as well as not-so-subtle ways in which you are targeted for persuasion each day. Understanding these strategies can help us to make better decisions in the future.

In this section you will:

- examine a model persuasive paragraph and essay
- learn about the components of persuasive writing
- analyze the structure of a persuasive paragraph and essay
- learn to identify and use persuasive techniques
- write a persuasive paragraph and essay.

Answer the following questions about academic life.

1. What are the advantages and disadvantages of taking a year off between high school and university?

2. Do you plan to take any time off before you graduate? If so, what will you do? If not, why not?

Persuasive Paragraph

Benefits of a Year Off

Many students are ill-prepared to make the transition from high school to university. Therefore, students should take a year off between high school and university. First of all, most students have known only academic life since their childhood. By the end of their 12 years of schooling, students are often tired of the routine. Time off provides a break from study in which young people can explore other interests before returning to academia to start their university career with renewed vigor and greater maturity. This time is also an opportunity to travel, which increases independence. This is very important for university life, where students are expected to take responsibility for their own learning. Finally, taking a year off gives students a chance to work. This can add valuable experience to the résumé as well as helping financially equip students for an increasingly expensive university education. In conclusion, a year off is a chance for young people to recharge, grow in independence and maturity, and gain valuable experience and cash to prepare them for college life and beyond.

Persuasive Essay

Benefits of a Year Off

Most Korean students expect to finish high school with the trauma of the Korean Scholastic Aptitude Test (KSAT). The intense stress of the exam and the pressure of the preceding years of study leave many students ill-prepared to embark on university life. The obvious solution is to take a year off between high school and university, and an increasing number of universities have formal policies that allow students to take a year off of study by deferring their placement. However, some argue that this is a waste of time and students are better off focusing on their education. While there is some logic to this argument, the potential benefits of a year off make it time well spent. Although this time off delays graduation and the start of a career, students should take a year out between school and university for their mental health, rich experiences, and the augmentation of their résumé.

First, by taking a year off students can recover from the long and arduous education marathon. By the time they finish high school, the average student will have spent around 15,000 hours in school: almost two full years, day and night. Most students have known nothing but the term/vacation cycle since starting school at the age of five. The final leg of this epic academic journey is the Korean Scholastic Aptitude Test (KSAT) which is seen as the most important exam that Korean students will ever face since it decides the students' fate in higher education. They are under great pressure to achieve a high ranking in order to attend a reputable university and gain the advantages of an elite education. This intensity can lead to what J. Lee et al. identify as "academic burnout" (16). Taking a year off is a way for students to take a thorough break from academia and recuperate from the stresses of the KSAT. This will, therefore, make them mentally better equipped to start their university studies with fresh enthusiasm for learning.

Not only is a year off a good opportunity to recuperate and reflect, but it is also a unique chance for young people to gain valuable life experience. One popular and rewarding way to spend a year off is to travel. It has long been popular for students to spend up to a year exploring the world before entering university. Since the 1960s, students have been taking advantage of time away from school to experience new cultures, learn languages, and gain valuable life experiences. Many universities regard a year off very highly, and there are organizations that help students make the most of their time through volunteer work and language programs in order to give them valuable skills and experiences to further appeal to top colleges and even employers. Thus, travel can be a good way to gain understanding of the world and develop skills that appeal to universities and employers.

For some, travel may be too expensive an option, but a year off can be a good chance to earn money, gain work experience, and develop valuable life skills. Another advantage of taking time away from school is that it is a chance to get a full-time job. According to the Korean Education Ministry, public university fees increased from 2.9 to 4.19 million won, or 44.5% between 2004 and 2009 (16). The report also shows that private university fees increased from 5.77 million won to 7.42 million won, or 28% over the same period. A year off gives students a chance to earn money to pay for some of these costs and reduce the burden on their family. An additional benefit is the opportunity to gain valuable experience and make useful contacts which are increasingly important in today's competitive job market. Finally, a year of working with adults is a good way for young people to learn about the expectations and realities of the adult world. Therefore, the experience helps them to mature and set realistic goals based on their knowledge of real-life.

In conclusion, high school graduates should take a year off before starting university in order to revive their enthusiasm for study, see the world, and improve their résumé. Some disagree, suggesting that the year would be better spent as a freshman student. However, many students suffer from academic burnout and benefit greatly from a year off. There are many advantages to taking time to see the world when one is young and free from responsibilities that come after graduation. Furthermore, a year off can be well spent working to earn money for tuition fees and gaining experience in a relevant field. Students taking a year off are better prepared for a successful future.

Activity 2

Answer the following questions about the essay.

1. In your own words, what is the writer's opinion?

   _____

   _____

2. What were the three reasons for his or her opinion?

   _____

   _____

3. What do you think is the strongest reason? Why?

   _____

   _____

4. Do you agree with the writer's opinion? Why or why not?

   _____

   _____

Fact vs. Opinion

In persuasive writing, writers usually present an opinion and then use a variety of strategies to convince the reader that the opinion is reasonable. Therefore, writers must understand the difference between fact and opinion. A fact is a verifiable truth or certainty: "The actor Christopher Lee played Count Dracula in nine different films." An opinion is a personal thought or position: "Christopher Lee was the best Count Dracula."

It is important to remember that the wording of facts and opinions is very important. For example, "Roger Moore is my favorite James Bond" is actually a fact about an opinion. In the same way, "My grandfather hates dentists" is a fact about my grandfather's opinion of dentists.

Activity 3

Read the following sentences, and identify which are facts (F) and which are opinions (O).

1. Lee, Sun Shin was born in Hanseong (now Seoul) in 1545.

2. The woolly rhinoceros lived in Asia and Europe until around 10,000 years ago.

3. Steve Jobs was the most important person of his generation.

4. In Shi'a culture, couples occasionally enter into temporary marriages in which they agree to a term of commitment from between one hour and 99 years.

5. Temporary marriage should be introduced into every culture.

6. Space colonies are the only way to prevent the extinction of our species.

7. Since more people are killed in horse racing than any other sport, horse racing should be banned.

8. The number of Internet users in China increased from 22 million to 450 million between 2000 and 2010.

9. Climate change is the biggest global issue these days.

10. My teacher thinks that students should take a year to work or travel after finishing high school and before starting university.

Persuasive Paragraph Structure

The persuasive paragraph follows the same structure as any other paragraph. It usually starts with an introductory sentence to give background information. It then has a topic sentence, which gives the writer's opinion. The body of the paragraph usually gives three reasons for the opinion. Finally, there is the conclusion in which the writer restates his or her opinion.

Introduction sentence: Give some brief background to your topic so the reader can understand your opinion.

Topic sentence: Write a sentence that gives your opinion in a clear, concise way.

Reason 1: What is the first reason for your opinion? How can you back this up?

Reason 2: Give the second reason for your opinion.

Reason 3: Give the third reason for your opinion.

Concluding sentence: Restate your opinion in different words.

Signpost See page 46 for more information on paragraph outlines.

Activity 4

Read the example persuasive paragraph on page 118 and complete the outline.

Topic: Year Off

Topic sentence: _____

Reason 1: _____

Reason 2: _____

Reason 3: _____

Concluding sentence: _____

Topic

When choosing a topic for a persuasive writing assignment, it is very important to consider two questions:

1. What are you interested in? You will probably write a better essay if you write on a topic you are passionate about.

2. What is the purpose of your writing? If you are writing an assignment, your teacher will probably give you some guidelines, such as a topic area or an imaginary audience. Think about what your teacher wants you to show them through your writing and select a topic that will help you to meet these goals. If you are writing for another purpose, think about your intended audience. Use appropriate language and terminology, and pick examples that will appeal to them.

Activity 5

Write a question for each of the following topics. Then answer one question and give three reasons for your answer.

Topic: Pets

Question: Should people in one room apartments keep pets?

Opinion (Thesis): People in small apartments should keep pets.

1. Pets are great companions. People in one room apartments are probably single and lonely.

2. Pets are entertaining. People can have more fun with a pet than watching television.

3. Small houses are good places for small pets, such as hamsters.

Plastic Surgery	Nuclear Power	The Death Penalty	Euthanasia

Topic: _____

Question: _____

Opinion: _____

Reason 1: _____

Reason 2: _____

Reason 3: _____

Persuasive Essay Structure

A five-paragraph persuasive essay contains the basic essay components: Introductory paragraph, body paragraphs, and concluding paragraph. The writer's opinion is given in the thesis statement, and it is supported with facts and evidence in the body paragraphs. The restated thesis in the conclusion gives the opinion one more time, along with a summary of the reasons.

Introductory paragraph: Include a hook, relevant background information, and finish with the thesis statement and opinion.

Body paragraphs: Give the reasons for your opinion. Back them up with evidence.

Concluding paragraph: Restate your opinion and give a strong summary of your reasons. Finish with a clear wrap-up sentence.

A good persuasive essay should:

- Begin with an appropriate hook
- Phrase the opinion as a strong statement
- Include qualifiers (e.g. "most" instead of "all", "usually" instead of "always")
- Include reasons that appeal to the intended reader
- Use facts to support the argument
- Give credible sources for supporting information
- Be logical and internally consistent
- Include a counterargument: Acknowledge the opposing viewpoint and refute it
- Restate the opinion in the conclusion
- Conclude memorably and have a clear wrap-up sentence

Seeing Both Sides

When writing a persuasive piece, good writers consider opposing opinions in order to present a more reasonable argument. It allows the writer to explain why opposing viewpoints are less reasonable than the one being argued for.

Activity 6

Choose one of the following opinions and write a list of ideas for and against it.

1. All captive animals should be released into the wild.

2. Young people should have plastic surgery to improve their appearance.

3. All university lectures should be broadcast online instead of being taught live in class.

4. Children should be homeschooled.

5. The subway is better than the bus.

For	Against

Counterarguments

A counterargument is an opposing viewpoint the writer uses to address the concerns or doubts of the reader and then refutes them with sound reasoning. The advantages of including a counterargument in your persuasive writing are:

1. It shows that you have considered opposing viewpoints and opinions.
2. It directly confronts possible objections the reader may have.
3. It shows that you are a considerate writer and therefore makes your opinion more compelling.

There are four steps to writing a counterargument:

Step 1: Identify an opposing viewpoint.

Some people argue that homeschooling isolates children from their peers.

Objection phrases
One might object…
A possible objection might be…
Some people argue that…

Step 2: Comment on the validity or strength of this viewpoint.

It is true that homeschooled children interact with fewer children during the day, but…

Concession phrases

It is true that…, but…   This is rarely true…
While this is sometimes true…   It has never been shown to be the case…
This may be true in some cases…   It is not actually the case that…

Step 3: Provide your point of view (refutation).

Refutation phrases

However, …   This is not applicable because…
It is also true that…
Studies show that…

Step 4: Provide a strong reason or evidence to support your opinion over the opposing opinion.

… homeschooling is often done with groups of children from several families. Studies show that they form stronger relationships than children who interact in the more populous school environment. Furthermore, there are plenty of opportunities for outside activities in the community, including sports teams and clubs.

Activity 7

Write a counterargument for the following opinion.

People who do military service should not have to pay university tuition fees.

Opposing viewpoint: _____

Concession: _____

Refutation: _____

Support: _____

Wrap-up Sentence

The final sentence in the essay can be used to make a final comment about your topic or opinion. However, in a persuasive essay, it is sometimes necessary to finish with a "call to action."

For example, for the topic "The benefits of flossing," the action would be to buy some dental floss and floss each day after meals. If your essay is persuasive enough, the reader is likely to do it.

Signpost See page 79 for more information on concluding memorably.

Activity 8

Write some actions to match the following topics.

Topic	Action
The AIDS epidemic	_____
Abandoned animals	_____
Vivisection (Animal testing)	_____
The disabled	_____
The environment	_____

Activity 9

Write a persuasive essay.

7 Reports

Reports are another form of writing which students may be required to complete at university. Typically used in business, and in social and natural sciences, they are used to analyze a situation and/or to present practical research findings in an accurate, objective, and complete manner. The author must apply business or science knowledge previously learned in order to suggest improvements or conclusions to problem-based situations, observations, or empirical investigations.

Reports can use an inductive or deductive structure depending on the intended audience. This structure dictates the order in which the information is presented. Deductive reports move from general to specific information and are for an audience who does not have a lot of time to read the whole document. Inductive reports move from specific issues to more general summarizations. These reports are directed towards an audience who has time to read the whole document, and may require a natural flow of information from the evidence to the recommendations in order convince the reader of a controversial topic. This chapter focuses on inductive report writing as it is the most common style in academics.

In this section you will:

- examine the difference between essays and reports
- analyze the organizational pattern of reports with particular focus on either business or science
- examine why critical thinking and specialized vocabulary are important for report writing
- write a report.

Choose an essay and a report from the textbook. In general, what are the similarities and differences between reports and essays?

Similarities	Differences

Critical Thinking: An Important Skill

Report writing requires the writer to be critical of the study in question, and therefore critical thinking is a vital skill to obtain. Having the skills required to analyze and evaluate data in different situations and the ability to read between the lines and think outside the box will help you to identify flaws and limitations, and how these may affect the results. Critical thinking also helps the overall report to be more credible to your audience.

By asking and answering a series of questions, you will be more critical in terms of writing the description, analysis, and evaluation. In the description, one needs to help readers understand the topic by using *who*, *when*, *where*, and *what* type questions. On the other hand, *how*, *why*, and *what if* questions are used to examine relationships and give reasons in the analysis. Lastly, in the evaluating section you must judge the success or failure of something and its implementations, and therefore should focus on what next or so what questions. These will help lead you to the conclusion and recommendations.

Activity 2

Which questions go with which stage?

Who is affected?

What does this mean?

Why was it done?

Is it successful?

What next?

What can we learn from this?

What are the alternatives?

What is the context?

What needs to be done now?

How does it occur?

What are the implications?

Does it meet the criteria?

What if this or that factor were added or removed?

How does one factor affect the other?

Why not something else?

What is the main point?

Introduction	Analysis	Evaluation

Business Reports

Writing business reports is an important skill to develop as they are used in the business world to investigate a problem or situation. These reports contain recommendations with regards to fixing the existing issues. They are very different from essays, so they do not follow the same format. Even though they are in paragraph form, they are not structured like an essay. Full grammatically correct sentences are used, but in addition, the use of bullet points, numbered lists and tables are very common. The other similarity is that a works cited or references page must be included; however, reports also add an appendix, a title page, and a table of contents. It is important to note that there are many different report styles and structures, so it is vital that you always check with your professor regarding which style they require.

A business report should contain:

- a title page
- an executive summary (100 words)
- a table of contents (if the paper is longer than 6 pages)
- an introduction (100 words)
- a findings and discussion section (300 words)
- a conclusion (150 words)
- a recommendations section (200 words)
- a limitations and assumptions section (50 words)
- a Works Cited page
- appendices.
  *Approx. based on a 1000 word limit

Title Page

The title page should include your name, student ID, professor's name, class number, and the title of the report. The title should be brief but descriptive. Unlike the other pages in your report, this is not given a page number.

Executive Summary

The executive summary contains the report's purpose, conclusions, and main recommendations. This gives the reader a sense of what the report will cover and the key findings. It follows the same outline as the overall report starting with the aim of the investigation, problem or issue, methods used to investigate the issue, conclusions, recommendations, and finishes with limitations.

Activity 1

Read and answer the following questions.

Who is this report for?

_____

What is the main issue?

_____

How was information collected?

_____

What is the main recommendation?

_____

The aim of this report is to analyze the issues concerning the advertising campaign for the new LEO Phoenix drone and offer suggestions for improving the campaign. The existing advertising campaign was found to have used footage that was not legally approved for commercial uses. Data was collected from a review of the existing materials, interviews with members of the Asian advertising department, and analysis of the contracts made for the initial filming schedule. LEO needs to act swiftly to alleviate the loss of brand value, release new promotional footage and advertising materials, and reduce the negative impact to the future sales of the Phoenix with a clear and concise new message.

Signpost See page 216-221 for more information on paraphrasing and summarizing.

Activity 2

Put the sentences in order to construct an executive summary.

_____In addition, up-to-date literature on advertising was taken into consideration, as were the opinions of the existing advertising manager.

_____The existing advertising campaign has been found inadequate to target the potential millennial customer base.

_____The results indicated that there is a significant gap between current advertising media and those used by the target customers.

_____The aim of this report is to propose a new advertising and media framework.

_____Recommendations

- Increase the budget for online advertising by 10% while decreasing print advertising by 3%.

- Reeducate staff members on up to date marketing strategies.

- Create an incentive plan to inspire more creative forms of advertising.

_____A new advertising project could increase product awareness in the core customer base by 13% leading to an overall profit margin increase of 5%.

_____Qualitative data was collected from a survey conducted through 30 interviews. The participants, aged 20-25, were randomly chosen from an existing database.

_____It is unclear how this will affect the overall yearly budget as it will depend if in-house or out sourced training occurs.

Introduction

The introduction sets the scene for the audience. It follows the general flow of an essay introduction but also includes a description of the reported issue and the aim of the report. The focus is to give background information to your reader regarding how the problem originated and why the problem needs to be addressed.

Activity 3

Read the introduction, follow the directions, and answer the questions below.

On July 5th, 2019, a new advertising campaign was screened for the LEO, Phoenix drone. Also promoted as 'Phoenix the fun maker', this drone is an updated version of the LEO Alpha, and the new drone was expected to help drive sales for LEO in the domestic market. However, the footage from the advertising campaign was deemed to have used footage from the Jeju area that was filmed without the appropriate legal consent. The Korean Ministry of Culture, Sports, and Tourism claimed that they had only issued Sellout, the advertising campaign production company, permission to shoot documentary footage. Therefore, the commercial was not legally allowed for commercial use.

1. Underline the <u>when</u>

2. Circle the (who)

3. Put a box around the [what]

4. What was the main problem?

_____

5. What led to the problem?

_____

Findings and Discussion

The findings and discussion is the most important section and requires an in-depth analysis in order to show the reader how you obtained the conclusion and recommendations. The findings should use exact information, figures, and data to give evidence and support for your recommendations. This can be shown through various tables and/or diagrams that are directly integrated into the text or placed in the appendix. For ease of use, the discussion is typically divided into sections which are numbered and named appropriately.

Headings and Subheadings

Excellent headings and subheadings help to guide the reader effectively to the information that they are searching for. Each heading and subheading should be descriptive and indicate to the reader what the following text is about. You should use numbered titles to describe the information that follows (e.g. 1.2 Establish communication systems). Make sure you have unity between a heading and its subordinating text. Regarding grammar, headings, and subheadings, follow sentence capitalization rules such as capitalizing only the first word and proper nouns. Use different font styles such as bold and italics to easily distinguish headings from subheadings.

Signpost See page 35-36 for more information on unity.

Activity 4

Fill in the blanks with numbered subheadings. Make sure it is descriptive.

With high expectations for the new drone, LEO was readying the promotion and campaign for Phoenix, having initially previewed it in March at the 2019 Technology Expo. Then on July 3rd, the first images were released and two days later, the commercial was shown in theatres across South Korea. The drone was expected to begin pre-sales in July and then officially be released in August, and then it was expected to be released in America in 2020.[1] The Phoenix had high expectations and was looking to be positioned near the high-price end of the videography models.

1   Write, Terry. "2020 LEO Phoenix the Fun Maker Revealed." Droblog, June 10, 2019. https://www.droblog.com/2019/06/10/LEO-phoenix-fun-maker/.

The advertising campaign was produced by an external company, Sellout. The issues arose after its initial screenings when it received criticism from the Korean government. The Ministry of Culture, Sports and, Tourism granted Sellout permission to film a documentary about Jeju in March under the condition that the broadcaster would not use footage filmed there for commercial use. The Ministry threatened to take legal action against Sellout if they continued to use the advertisement, and the campaign cost 1 billion won to produce.[2]

Once notified about the incorrect use of Jeju footage, LEO chose to pull all screenings of the advertisement. As a result, LEO had to delay the launch date for the new drone, although it ended up being delayed only two days.[3] Currently, new advertising materials are being shot without the use of the Sellout footage, and the payments to that company will not be made in full. LEO was under the impression that full permission to film in Jeju for commercial purposes had been received and is currently reviewing the future use of Sellout for advertising production purposes.

Tables and Figures

Business reports often use tables and figures to illustrate important information. Tables are used to show numbers and/or text. Figures are often a visualization of the information shown in the form of a graph or chart image. Place tables and figures critical to understanding the discussion directly in the text and other supporting material in the appendix. This depends on whether the reader needs to refer to it while they are reading to truly understand the discussion, or if the tables and figures could be used but are not needed. If the reader is required to refer to the table or figure then it should be included within the text. If the table or figure is included in the text, the writer must directly refer to it by name and include only the key points (e.g., Table 1 illustrates . . .). Readers should not be left guessing why you added the table or figure and how it fits into your discussion. Figures must help clarify the ideas you are discussing, and they must be clear enough to be understood without referring to the text.

The table or figure must be positioned two lines below the text that mentions it. All tables and figures (included appended ones) must be labeled with a title and number.

2   "LEO's New Phoenix Drone Launch Delayed." The Korea Business Weekly, June 18, 2019. http://www.kbw.co.kr/2019/06/Pheonix-launch/.

3   Stukle, James. "LEO Phoenix Masterpiece Concept Debuts Autonomous Flight Modes." Droblog, May 01, 2019. https://www.droblog.com /2019/05/01/LEO-Phoenix-masterpiece-seoul-drone-show/.

Figure 1 shows the total LEO sales in the United States over summer 2019, with April to June confirmed and showing a steady increase.[4] For July, August, and September, the expected sales show a strong decline, in part due to the issues concerning the delay in the promotion and release of the Phoenix.

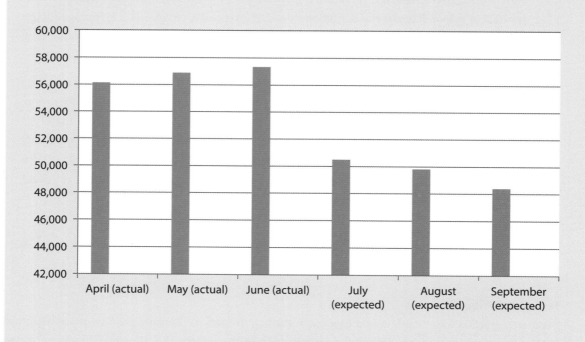

Figure 1. Total USA LEO Drone Sales

Signpost See page 173 for more information on capitalization.

4   "Sales Results." IR Library | IR | Company | PR LEO. Accessed July 30, 2019. http://pr.leo.com/en/ company/ir/ir-library/sales-results.do.

Activity 5

Give a title and number to the charts and figures below.

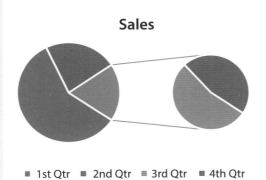

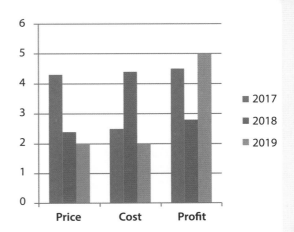

| Stock available | • Print invoice
• Shipping |

| Stock not available | • Advise marketing
• Inform customer |

Year	Average female wage	Average male wage
2016	$350	$500
2017	$388	$515
2018	$419	$524
2019	$468	$536

Activity 6

Describe the main points while referring to the table/figure.

1.

2.

3.

4.

5.

Conclusion

A report conclusion summarizes and interprets the main points in the findings and discussion. No new information should be added in this section, and the writer must remain objective. Remember to link the conclusion to the issue or problem that needs to be solved.

The difficulty in this situation is that the campaign was made external to LEO and the subsidiary companies, and the timing could not have been worse. From a consumer's perspective, the fact that it was made externally will not matter as it is the LEO brand that will be deemed at fault. The fact that the advertising campaign was removed during the critical period is expected to have an impact on the demand and sales for the Phoenix, although credit should go to the swift response and clear source of the issue concerning the commercial. All materials in any advertising productions need to adhere not just to legal requirements, but to all laws, norms, and social guidelines; and closer attention must be made to ensure similar incidents do not occur in the future. In summary, the main focus is to reduce the damage done to the 2019 sales of the LEO Phoenix in South Korea, and ideally react within the timelines stated previously in this report.

Recommendations

The difference between a conclusion and a recommendation is the sense of time. Recommendations are focused on the future whereas conclusions concentrate on the past or present. After analyzing the situation, you should be able to make recommendations on the direction which the company should take to overcome the problem. Be very specific when making these recommendations, and let the reader know what action the company should take. Make sure to number and arrange the recommendations from most to least important. There is usually no answer that is 100% correct, but rather there are several solutions to the problem or situation.

Overall, LEO is looking to recover and move on from this campaign to ensure minimal damage is done to the reputation of the company and the sales of the Phoenix. This can be achieved by following the below recommendations.

- Issue an immediate apology regarding the footage.
- Ensure the staff members involved were officially reprimanded and reminded of the appropriate contracts and legal implications of footage and all advertising materials.
- Withhold a proportion of the fees due to DKEP, and establish a 12-month period whereby LEO will not use this company for any promotions.
- Develop and produce a new adverting campaign prior to August's official Phoenix launch.
- Involve Innocean (a new advertising company) in future advertising campaigns for all LEO brands.

Activity 7

Mark the conclusions with a C and the recommendations with an R.

1. Gender directly affects wage earnings.

2. Provide an opportunity for further reeducation.

3. Publish an incentive program.

4. An increase in advertising lead to a 10% increase in customers.

5. Install a new budget planning network.

6. A work life balance helped increase productivity.

Activity 8

Write a recommendation for the problems below.

1. Air pollution in South Korea

_____

2. Students not wanting to study English

_____

3. Increase in aging population

_____

4. Students cheating during exams

_____

5. A new business competitor has built their shop right next to yours

_____

Limitations vs Assumptions

Limitations and assumptions are important as they affect the inferences made in the conclusion and recommendations. By adding them, you make the reader aware that you understand the study is not perfect.

Limitations are potential flaws in the report due to things outside the researchers' control. These occur all the time, and are unavoidable, but by stating them you can demonstrate your understanding of the research procedure. For example, the overall budget was lower due to limited funding and could have reduced the participant numbers needed for a successful study.

Assumptions are aspects in the study that anyone can guess are true. For example, if someone owned a dog then people would assume that they liked dogs. If you asked someone a simple question, people would assume the answer would be truthful and not a lie.

This business report was written utilizing all available information, but various aspects could not be independently verified. Facts concerning the correspondence between Sellout, the Korean Ministry of Culture, Sports, and Tourism, and the Jeju governing body, could not be 100% confirmed, although the communications seemed consistent. Another area concerned how many movie theatres the Phoenix advertisements were screened at, which may have had an impact on the reaction, but decisions were made based on an assumed number.

Activity 9

Fill in the table below.

A questionnaire	A test	A small sample size
Limitations:	Limitations:	Limitations:
Assumptions:	Assumptions:	Assumptions:

Bibliography

Essays contain a Works Cited page. Similarly business reports need to have a bibliography page to show the reader where you collected your information. Every entry should be mentioned in an in-text citation and written in alphabetical order.

Signpost See page 237 for more information on how to create a Works Cited page

Appendices

Your appendix should consist of tables, figures, raw data, questionnaire details, transcripts, and other information that are secondary and may clutter the main parts of your report. Each should be placed in the order which they are mentioned in the text and have their own title such as Appendix A and Appendix B. This helps the reader refer to the information within the content of the report (e.g., see Appendix A for more information).

Checklist

Overall

Objectives clearly addressed ☐

Formatting and layout ☐

Audience

Tone ☐

Style ☐

Executive summary

Complete (will readers understand it without reading the report?) ☐

Introduction

Is clear ☐

Provides purpose and objectives ☐

Explains context ☐

Explains relevant issues ☐

Describes any limitations ☐

Describes any assumptions ☐

Mentions major findings ☐

Identifies relevant theories ☐

Discussion

Is clear	☐
Is analytical	☐
Discusses issues	☐
Forms a foundation for your recommendations	☐
Contains headings and subheadings	☐
Tables/figures are titled and formatted	☐
Tables/figures are referred to within the	☐

Recommendations

Uses subheadings	☐
Are listed in order (chronological or level of importance)	☐

Limitations and assumptions

Scope and data	☐
Participants	☐

Bibliography (Referencing)

Works Cited page	☐
In-text citations	☐
Formatting	☐

Appendices

All resources have a title	☐
Listed in order as mentioned in the text	☐

Social Science Reports

Social science reports document procedures and findings of practical research, so they can be compared to other studies and replicated.

A social science report should contain:

- Title page
- Abstract
- Introduction
- Methods
- Discussion
- References
- Appendix

Although research is not a linear process, it generally follows these steps:

1. Generate a research question.
2. Write introduction and methods.
3. Conduct the study.
4. Write discussion, references, and appendix.
5. Write the abstract.

Look at the following chart to see how an essay and social science report are structured.

Essay	Social Science Report

Introduction paragraph
- Hook
- Background
- Thesis statement

Introduction
- Background
- Literature review
- Hypothesis

Funnel

Body paragraph 1
- Topic sentence
- Supporting details
- Concluding sentence

Methods
- Participants
- Instrumentation
- Procedure

Body paragraph 2
- Topic sentence
- Supporting details
- Concluding sentence

Results
- Objective summary of data

Body paragraph 3
- Topic sentence
- Supporting details
- Concluding sentence

Discussion
- Was the hypothesis supported?
- Flaws and limitations

Conclusion paragraph
- Restate overview
- Summarize main points
- Conclude memorably

Abstract
Summarize:
- Purpose
- Methods
- Results

» The Introduction

The introduction provides readers with sufficient background to understand your study's context without needing outside resources. It is structured like a funnel, so it begins with general background information, summarizes past studies, and ends with the purpose of your study in the form of a hypothesis.

Signpost For more information about funnels, see page 64.

Literature Review

Literature review describes theoretical frameworks that underlie your study. It also summarizes hypotheses, methods, and results of past relevant research. Be selective by only including literature that embeds your study within your research's scope. These guidelines may help you find relevant literature.

a. Start with search engines such as Google Scholar or your university library.

b. Type research related keywords in the search field. If the search query does not produce pertinent articles, use alternative keywords.

c. Read titles and abstracts to decide which articles are relevant to your study.

d. When reviewing articles:

    1. record the title of the article, source, methods, and results,

    2. skim through the literature review to find prior relevant studies, and

    3. use search tools such as Google Scholar to find cited by and related articles.

Keep track of all your sources by recording information in a table. This will help with citations.

Article	Source	Methods	Results
No More FOMO: Limiting Social Media Decreases Loneliness and Depression	Journal of Social and Clinical Psychology (Guilford Press)	Experiment of limiting social media on an intervention group / Well-being measured through a series of self-reported surveys	Limiting social media use reduced mental health issues.
Dependency on Smartphone Use and Its Association with Anxiety in Korea	Public Health Reports (Sage Journals)	Statistical analysis of smartphone use, anxiety, and dependency through self-reported surveys and questionnaires	Social media use was one of the main contributing factors to smartphone dependency and an increase in smartphone dependency increased the likelihood of reported anxiety.

Activity 1

Choose one question. Find two relevant articles using the guidelines above and record article, source, methods, and results in the table below.

1. How does lack of sleep affect university students' academic performance?

2. What is more effective for taking lecture notes: pen and paper or a notebook computer?

3. Can walking make a person more creative?

Article	Source	Methods	Results

Activity 2

After completing the table in Activity 1, discuss these questions with a partner or in small groups.

1. Do the articles reference common studies?

2. Which articles are cited the most?

3. Are the study results conflicting or converging?

What Is a Hypothesis?

A hypothesis is a predictive statement answering a question your study is attempting to address and should be informed from the literature review.

What Makes a Good Hypothesis?

A good hypothesis has all of the following attributes:

1. It is a predictive statement about the relationship between two things

Good example:
Note-taking with a tablet and stylus is as effective as pen and paper for understanding a 50-minute lecture on the history of Sungkyunkwan.

This statement contains two variables: Note-taking with a tablet and stylus and understanding a 50-minute lecture on the history of Sungkyunkwan. The predictive aspect is as effective as pen and paper.

Poor example:
Note taking with a tablet and stylus is good.

There is only one variable (Note-taking with a tablet and stylus), and there is no prediction.

2. It is specific

Good example:

Note-taking with a tablet and stylus is as effective as pen and paper for understanding a 50-minute lecture on the history of Sungkyunkwan.

This statement is specific in terms of note taking instrumentation and the lecture's time length and topic.

Poor example:

Tablets and styluses are better than notebook computers for taking notes.

The context of note-taking is unspecified, and "better" is not defined.

3. It is testable

Good example:

Note-taking with a tablet and stylus is as effective as pen and paper for understanding a 50-minute lecture on the history of Sungkyunkwan.

Comparing lecture comprehension test results of participants taking notes with a tablet and stylus versus pen and paper can test the hypothesis.

Poor example: too broad.

Tablets and styluses can be used to take lecture notes.

This is a simple fact. There is nothing to test.

Activity 3

Look at the following hypotheses. For each one, state whether it is a good hypothesis or a poor one. If it is poor, explain why.

Example: Rock music is better than K-pop.

It is a poor hypothesis because it is not specific. "Better" is not defined.

1. People who go to university become smarter.

   _____

   _____

2. The introduction of the smartphone has increased the number of traffic accidents in Korea.

   _____

   _____

3. Increasing cigarette taxes decreases the smoking rate.

   _____

   _____

4. Entrepreneurs who prefer working early in the morning are more likely to establish successful companies than those who prefer working later in the day.

   _____

   _____

5. People who have a little knowledge about politics are more likely to overestimate their political knowledge.

   _____

   _____

6. Thor, the Norse god of thunder, does not exist.

   _____

   _____

7. Extra Sensory Perception (ESP) only works with true believers.

_____

_____

8. University students who habitually eat three meals a day earn higher grades than those who habitually skip meals.

_____

_____

9. Sugar influences children's hyperactive behavior.

_____

_____

10. High school students who are forced to partake in community service volunteer less as adults.

_____

_____

Activity 4

Read the sample report introduction and answer the following questions.

1. Which paragraph(s) provide(s) general background information?

2. What kinds of sources were used for background information (news media or academic journals), and how many sources were used?

3. Which paragraph(s) review(s) past studies (i.e., literature review)?

4. How many and what kinds of sources were used for the literature review (news media or academic journals)?

5. Where is the hypothesis located? Is it a good or poor hypothesis? Why?

6. Explain how this introduction is structured like a funnel.

Social Media Use and Loneliness Among South Korean University Students

1   South Korea has the highest smartphone ownership rate in the world (Taylor & Silver, 2019) and is experiencing a conflicting relationship with these devices. Due to Korea's aging population, senior citizens are encouraged to use smartphones to help increase social participation to overcome loneliness. Private companies and local governments offer classes throughout the country to teach seniors how to use smartphones and social media. Some seniors have reported positive effects of social media through sharing family stories and hand drawn pictures, and following youth culture such as K-pop (S. Kim, 2019). In contrast, internet and smartphone addiction are concerns for South Korea's youth. The addiction rate for three to nine year olds and teenagers are 1.2% and 3.5% respectively. These represent extreme cases of children spending at least eight hours a day on their devices. Local governments have set up boot camps to help wean these children off their digital habits. Although they claim to have a success rate of 70 – 75%, they are too few in numbers to effectively address this problem ("How children interact," 2019).

2   According to a survey conducted by the Korea Information Society Development Institute, half of all Koreans use social media. The most active users are people in their twenties at 83.2 %, and Facebook and Kakao Story are the two most popular platforms at 34% and 27% respectively. Furthermore, users consume social media 20 to 40 times more on smartphones than on conventional computers (R. Kim, 2019).

3   Lee et al. (2016) studied the relationship between smartphone dependency and anxiety among South Korean undergraduate students. They collected information relating to smartphone use, anxiety, and dependency through self-reported surveys and questionnaires. They found that social media use was one of the main contributing factors to smartphone dependency and an increase in smartphone dependency increased the likelihood of reported anxiety.

4   This study aims to verify the results of the aforementioned study in a simplified way by examining the relationship between social media use and loneliness among young South Korean adults. It was predicted that undergraduate students who spent above average time on social media would report a higher degree of loneliness.

» Methods

Methods describe how you carried out your study and analyzed your results. Provide enough information to allow others to replicate your study. Write in the past tense, and use passive voice when necessary to avoid the first person.

> **Signpost** See page 191 for more information on the passive voice and page 201 for guidance on avoiding the first person.

Methods for social science reports typically study human behavior, so they contain the following sections:

Participants

The participants are a sample representation of a population under study. Give a detailed description of the population's demographic and a rationale for sample size. However, do not provide irrelevant or personal details that could disclose the identity of the participants.

Sample hypothesis – The number of years living in an English speaking country positively correlates with comprehension of English lectures.

Good example:
The participants included 20 students enrolled in a first year English course at a South Korean university. Ten students never lived abroad. The remaining students lived in the US: one year for three students, two years for four students, and five years for three students. The sample size is similar to other comparable studies (Cain, 2015; Kim, 2017; Lee, 2018).

All of the information is relevant to the study.

Poor example: Too vague.
The participants included 20 South Korean university students.

The description is missing important demographic information such as the number of years students lived in an English speaking country. Furthermore, there is no rationale for sample size.

Poor example: Too specific.
The participants included 20 students (12 females, 8 males) enrolled a first year English course during spring of 2019 at Sungkyunkwan University. The course number was GDSO01-A5. Ten students never lived abroad. The remaining students lived in the US: one year for three students, two years for four students, and five years for three students. The sample size is similar to other comparable studies (Cain, 2015; Kim, 2017; Lee, 2018).

Gender is irrelevant to the purpose of the study as are the name of the university, course code, and semester. Furthermore, this threatens the anonymity of the participants.

Instrumentation

Instrumentation refers to tools used for measuring such as surveys and questionnaires. One must consider their validity and reliability.

Validity is the gap between the actual and intended measurement. In other words, is your instrumentation measuring what you intend? If using a questionnaire, can the questions be misinterpreted?

Reliability is the measurement's consistency when repeated under similar conditions. For example, if you measured the length of a table numerous times and had consistent results, your measuring tape is reliable. On the other hand, your measuring tape would be unreliable if it yielded different successive measurements.

When possible, use tests, surveys, and questionnaires reported in past literature since their validity and reliability have been established. If you need to devise your own survey or questionnaire, state in the discussion section that its reliability and validity have not been established.

Signpost For more information about discussion in social science reports, see page 161.

Activity 5

With a partner, brainstorm limitations of participants and instrumentation such as surveys, tests, and questionnaires. Record your ideas below.

Activity 6

Compare your responses to Activity 5 with the ones below. Which limitations are common? Which ones are different?

- Self reported data might not be accurate.
- Participants may misunderstand survey questions or instructions.
- Too many survey questions may cause fatigue increasing the likelihood of careless responses.
- Self-selection bias may occur if the participants represent a group of people who opt-into a survey. This is more common in on-line surveys.
- Participants represent a narrow demographic of a population such as using university students in psychology research.
- The sample size of participants may be too small to obtain meaningful results.
- Participants may respond favorably, but not honestly, if they have a relationship with the researcher(s) such as a teacher surveying students or friends surveying friends. This is known as the halo effect.

Design Procedure

Describe the steps in enough detail for others to replicate your study. For example, explain the medium of a survey or questionnaire (i.e., online or paper), instructions given to the participants, and the time frame used for data collection.

Explain how you analyzed your results. Write this section before you conduct your study and stick to it when you carry out your analysis.

When collecting quantitative data, you will have a group of numbers referred to as a data set. A simple way of analyzing a data set is to calculate and report averages and standard deviations. The average is a number that represents a data set. The standard deviation is how much the numbers differ from each other in the data set. Although calculating averages and standard deviations by hand can be tedious, they can easily be calculated using formula cells in a spreadsheet.

For illustrative purposes, we will compare the averages and standard deviations of midterm results from two classes. Class A and Class B have five students each. The students ask their professor the average midterm results to see how well they did compared to other classmates.

Student	Class A	Student	Class B
Minsu	60	James	75
Jimin	80	Hyewon	85
Sunah	100	Iru	82
Anne	75	Jeongsu	78
Jae	86	Carrie	80
Average	80.2	Average	80.0
Standard Deviation	14.7	Standard Deviation	3.8

The professor reports an average midterm grade of 80% in both classes. Minsu and Anne from Class A, and James and Jeongsu from Class B are disappointed since they scored below average.

The professor notes that Class A has a wider spread of grades than Class B. This results in a larger standard deviation in Class A and a tighter standard deviation in Class B. In other words, Class A has a larger variation in midterm grades than Class B.

Activity 7

Read the following hypothesis:

Undergraduate students who spent above average time on social media would report a higher degree of loneliness.

Write a methods plan by considering participants, instrumentation, design procedure, and analysis.

Activity 8

Read the sample report methods and answer the following questions.

1. How many participants were enrolled in the study, what is the justification for this number, and what are some limitations?

2. What type of instrumentation was used to collect the data? What are some limitations of the instrumentation?

3. How many participants were dropped from the study, and why?

4. How was the data analyzed?

5. Would you be able to repeat this study by reading the methods section? Why or why not?

Methods

Participants

This study consisted of 21 undergraduate students at a South Korean university who were enrolled in a first year academic English writing course. The mean age was 19.5 years. The sample size was based on convenience, as the study needed to be completed within one academic semester.

Instrumentation

Participants recorded daily social media use on a self-reported survey. Social media was defined as applications such as Facebook, Instagram, Kakao Story, Snapchat, and Twitter.

The Revised UCLA Loneliness Scale was used to measure loneliness. Originally developed by Russell, Peplau, and Cutrona (1980), it is widely used and has high internal consistency and concurrent validity, meaning that its validity compared well to prior conventional tests. The questionnaire contains 20 statements such as "I am no longer close to anyone", "I feel left out", and "There are people who really understand me" on a scale of 1 (never) to 4 (often).

Procedure

Participants recorded and emailed daily social media usage along with the loneliness survey over four days. Although they received daily reminders via text message to minimize participation attrition, one participant stopped sending emails after two days and was omitted from the study. The average daily social media use of all participants was calculated to classify the participants into two groups: above average social media use and below average social media use. Averages and standard deviations of the loneliness scale were compared for both groups.

How similar and different are the sample report methods to the methods you wrote in Activity 7?

» Results

Summarize your data in an objective way and relate it back to your hypothesis. Use these guidelines to help you organize your data systematically.

1. State what is measured.
2. Summarize quantitative data and comment on trends. Although not mandatory, quantitative data can be illustrated using figures, tables, and charts. Present averages and standard deviations when applicable.
3. Summarize important qualitative data.
4. State whether the data supports the hypothesis. Reserve any interpretation and explanation for the discussion.

Activity 10

Read the sample report results and answer the following questions.

a) How is the data represented?

b) Does the data support the hypothesis? Why or why not?

Results

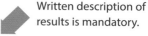

Written description of results is mandatory.

The average time spent on social media for all participants was 157 minutes per day. Thus, nine participants reported above average social media use ranging from 163 minutes to 235 minutes per day. The remaining participants were categorized as below average social media use, although one participant in this group was at the average of 157 minutes per day of social medial consumption. The average loneliness score for above average social media use was 57 with a standard deviation of deviation of 8. The average loneliness score for below average social media use was 47 with a standard deviation of 5.

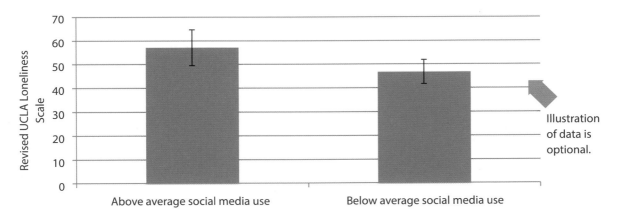

Figure 1. Social Media Users and Modified UCLA Loneliness Score

As shown in Figure 1, participants who reported above average social media use had higher loneliness scores than those who reported below average social media use.

Activity 11

Look at the chart below. The Subjective Happiness Scale is based on a 7 point Likert scale where 1 represents not very happy and 7 represents very happy. There are 80 participants (41 dog owners and 39 cat owners). Describe the data in the graph, but do not provide any interpretation. Use the sample report results in Activity 10 as a guide.

Lyubomirsky, S., & Lepper, H. S. (1999). A measure of subjective happiness: Preliminary reliability and construct validation. *Social Indicators Research*, 46(2), 137-155.

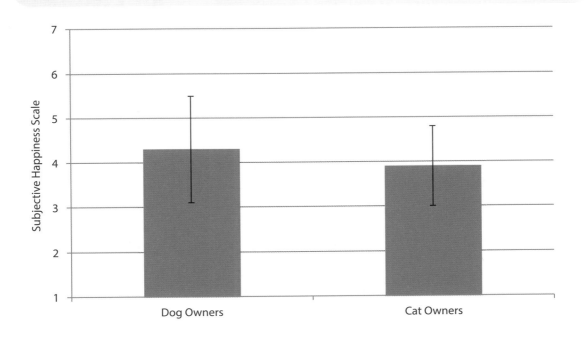

» Discussion

The discussion follows a reverse funnel from specific to general. Start with your hypothesis and state whether it is supported by the results. Explain why the results confirm or disconfirm the hypothesis. Furthermore, explain how the results conform to that of prior studies. It is important to express caution when making inferences without clear evidence.

Signpost See Precision on page 208 for more information about expressing caution.

Be critical of your study by identifying flaws and limitations, and how this may affect the results. By doing so, your readers will view your writing as more credible. Flaws may originate from reliability and validity issues, inadequate sample size, and/or random versus self-selected participants.

End the discussion with recommendations for follow up studies if your report has broader implications.

Activity 12

Read the sample report discussion and answer the following questions.

1. What are similarities or differences in the results of the study to the results reported by Lee et al. (2016)?

2. Did the author of the sample report attempt to explain why the results were similar or different from past literature? Is the author 100% confident in their explanation? What language does the author use to express their confidence? Why is this important?

3. Compare and contrast the limitations the author identified to your answers in Activity 8, Question 2.

4. What recommendations does the author make for future studies? What other recommendations could you make for follow-up research?

Discussion

The results confirm the hypothesis and are in line with results reported by Lee et al. (2016). They stated that participants who used smartphones primarily for social media, entertainment, and Internet searches had higher smartphone dependency than those who predominantly used smartphones for calls and other telephone-related functions. Furthermore, users consume social media on smartphones 20 to 40 times more than on conventional computers (R. Kim, 2019), thereby increasing smartphone dependency. The results of this study suggest that loneliness may contribute to an increase in social media use and smartphone dependency.

This study has some critical limitations. First, the sample size was based on convenience, so it may be too small to capture real trends. In addition, self-reporting social media use may not reflect actual usage. Next, no causal correlation can be established. For instance, it is unclear if lonely people tend to use more social media, if social media makes people feel lonelier because they are comparing themselves with others, or an outside factor not considered in this study increases loneliness and social media use. Finally, because the study was limited to undergraduate students in Seoul, the results cannot be generalized to the broader Korean population.

Further studies should be performed on Korea's elderly population to determine if social media is useful in reducing loneliness and depression as claimed in the media (S. Kim, 2019).

Activity 13

Look at the chart in Activity 11 and answer the following questions regarding the hypothesis below.

Dog owners are happier than cat owners.

1. Do the results confirm the hypothesis above? Why or why not?

2. What potential study flaws can you identify?

3. What recommendations would you make for future research?

» References

Similar to essays, social science reports need to have a page near the end of the paper to show the reader where you collected your information. Every entry should be mentioned in an in-text citation and written in alphabetical order. APA style is commonly used for formatting, citations, and references.

Signpost More information about APA formatting can be found at the Purdue Online Writing Lab at https://owl.purdue.edu/owl/research_and_citation/apa_style/apa_style_introduction.html

Activity 14

Number the references from 1 to 7. How many times does each reference appear in the following sections of the sample report?

1. Introduction – See Activity 4 on page 151.

2. Methods – See Activity 8 on page 157.

3. Results – See Activity 10 on page 158.

4. Discussion – See to Activity 12 on page 161.

References

How children interact with digital media. (2019, January 3). *The Economist*. Retrieved from https://www.economist.com/special-report/2019/01/03/how-children-interact-with-digital-media

Kim, R. (2019, June 9). 1 in 2 Koreans use social media: survey. *The Korea Times*. Retrieved from http://www.koreatimes.co.kr/www/culture/2019/06/703_270309.html

Kim, S. (2019, January 3). Aging South Koreans find new ways to communicate using social media. *ABC News*. Retrieved from https://abcnews.go.com/International/aging-south-koreans-find-ways-communicate-social-media/story?id=60085476

Lee, K. E., Kim, S. H., Ha, T. Y., Yoo, Y. M., Han, J. J., Jung, J. H., & Jang, J. Y. (2016). Dependency on smartphone use and its association with anxiety in Korea. *Public Health Reports*, 131(3), 411-419.

Russell, D., Peplau, L. A., & Cutrona, C. E. (1980). The revised UCLA Loneliness Scale: concurrent and discriminant validity evidence. *Journal of Personality and Social Psychology*, 39(3), 472.

Taylor, K., & Silver, L. (2019, February 5). Smartphone Ownership Is Growing Rapidly Around the World, but Not Always Equally. *Pew Research Center*. Retrieved from https://www.pewresearch.org/global/2019/02/05/smartphone-ownership-is-growing-rapidly-around-the-world-but-not-always-equally/

» Appendices

Your appendix should consist of tables, figures, raw data, questionnaire details, transcripts, and other information that is supplementary and may clutter the main parts of your report. Each should be placed in the order which they are mentioned in the text and have its own title such as Appendix A or Appendix B. This helps the reader refer to the information within the content of the report (e.g., see Appendix A for more information).

» Title Page

The title page will be the first page in your report and should include your name, student ID, professor's name, class number, and the title of the report. It should be brief but descriptive. Unlike the other pages in your report, this is not given a page number.

» Abstract

Although the abstract will be the first section that appears in your report, it should be the last thing that you write because it is a condensed version of your report limited to 250 words. It summarizes important information to help readers decide if they want to read the entire paper. It follows the same outline as the overall report starting with the purpose of the study, methods, results, and discussion. It should not reference outside research (literature review) or include new information.

Activity 15

Put the sentences in order to construct an abstract.

_____ Participants reported time spent on social media through a self-reported survey.

_____ Loneliness was measured using the Revised UCLA Loneliness Scale.

_____ An observational study was performed on undergraduate students (N=20) at a South Korean university to determine the effects of social media use on loneliness.

_____ Participants who reported above average social media use exhibited a greater degree of loneliness than those who reported below average social media use.

_____ This study suggests that reducing the use of social media could psychologically benefit young adults.

» Social Science Report Checklist

Abstract

Complete (will readers understand it without reading the report?) ☐

Introduction

Is clear ☐

Provides purpose and objectives ☐

Explains context ☐

Reviews relevant literature ☐

Gives a predictive, specific, and testable hypothesis ☐

Methods

Participants ☐

Instrumentation validity and reliability ☐

Design procedure ☐

Analysis ☐

Results

State what is measured ☐

Summarize quantitative data graphically ☐

Summarize important qualitative data ☐

State whether the data supports the hypothesis ☐

Are objective (descriptive, not interpretive) ☐

Tables/figures are titled and formatted ☐

Tables/figures are referred to within the report ☐

Discussion

Is clear	☐
Explains why the hypothesis is supported or not	☐
Relates results to past studies	☐
States limitations	☐
Provides suggestions for improving methodology	☐
Gives recommendations for future studies	☐

Citations

References page	☐
In-text citations	☐
APA Formatting	☐

Appendix

All resources have a title	☐
Listed in order as mentioned in the text	☐

Building Blocks

The basic foundation for all writing is the sentence. Grammatically sound sentences help writers to convey their message properly and accurately, but beyond grammar, there are also skills and techniques students can learn in order to enhance their writing and clarify their points. This section will help students to review basic grammar before moving into more complex skills and techniques students can use to improve their ability to write academically and objectively. A great deal of space is available for students to practice and perfect these skills before they try to bring them into longer paragraph and essay assignments.

This section does not have to be followed in a linear way. Rather, the information covered in these subsections can be incorporated into various forms of writing and contexts. The main point of this section is to help students develop the skills necessary to enrich their sentences and improve their overall writing techniques.

This section covers:

- Articles
- Capitalization
- Prepositions
- Conditionals
- Modals
- Adjectives
- Active vs. Passive Voice
- Comparatives and Superlatives
- Using Non-English Words in English
- Academic Writing Techniques
- Professional Writing Techniques
- Italics and Quotation Marks
- Logical Fallacies
- Paraphrasing and Summarizing

Articles

"A" and "an" are indefinite articles used to identify general nouns while "the" is the definite article which is used to refer to specific nouns.

Examples:

Niels Bohr was **a** Danish physicist. (one of many Danish physicists)
Niels Bohr was **the** physicist who first drew the structure of the atom. (the first to do something)

The students found **an** empty classroom, so they could study. (any room is fine)
The students could not find **the** classroom for their English class. (the specific room)

Indefinite Articles

"A" is used with words that sound like consonants while "an" is used with words that sound like vowels. In some words, vowels sound like consonants, so they need an "a" while in some words, consonants sound like vowels and should be preceded by an "an."

Examples:

When she was **a** sophomore, Jeong Ah only spent **an** hour on **an** eight page essay about **a** United Nations agency, so her professor gave her **an** "F."

Countable and Uncountable Nouns

"A" and "an" can only be used with countable nouns.

Countable	Uncountable	Both
Pear	Rice	Do you want **a chocolate**? (individual piece) I do not like **chocolate**. (in general)
Dollar	Money	He does not have **a hair** on his head. (individual strand) She just dyed her **hair** red. (whole head of hair)
Horse	Love	Is there **an extra room** in International Hall? (classroom) Do you have **room** in your car for me? (space)
Pen	Information	Is there **a light** in each room? (light fixture) Our new house has more **light**. (natural light)
Table	Equipment	**A scary experience** happened today. (occurrence) I have enough **experience** for this job. (general)

Examples:

If you have a pen, I will write down information about equipment you can buy to make homemade chocolate.

» Definite Articles

Like many areas of English grammar, there are some exceptions in how definite articles are used. Nevertheless, "the" is usually used in the following situations:

Use	Examples
Something previously mentioned	There is an unoccupied chair, but the chair looks broken.
Something specific or unique	The professor for this class just arrived.
A group of people identified by an adjective or a population as a whole	the unemployed, the Spanish
Instruments	the piano
Superlatives	the fastest
Plural names of groups of people and places	the Kims, the Netherlands
Country names including 'republic' and 'united'	the Republic of Ireland, the United Kingdom
Buildings (unless the first word is the name of a place)	the Blue House
Oceans, seas, rivers, canals, gulfs, peninsulas, deserts	the Pacific Ocean, the Black Sea, the Amazon, the Panama Canal
Mountain, island, or lake groups	the Himalayas, the Canary Islands, the Connecticut Lakes
Geographical regions, points on the globe, location	the West, the Equator, Gwangju is in the southern part of Korea.

Do not use "the" in the following situations:

Use	Examples
Most languages, nationalities	English, Australian
Continents, most countries, states/provinces	Europe, Morocco, British Columbia
Buildings (if the first word is the name of a place)	Seoul Liberty Building
Cities/towns, streets	Incheon, Main Street
Bays, parks, individual mountains, islands, or lakes	James Bay, Hyde Park, Bukhan Mountain, Easter Island, Lake Louise
Directions (when comparing two places)	Nepal is north of India.

💡 Grammar Tip

Using Non-English Words

Non-English words usually follow the same countable/non countable rules.

Activity 1

Correct the articles in the following sentences.

1. Before going on a hike, remember to pack a water, the chocolate bars, and map.

2. Young children should learn the Korean before they learn second language.

3. At the pet shop beside the Summer Hill Park, there were a snakes, a iguana, and the turtle.

4. The Seoul is located on Korean Peninsula in South Korea, which is also called Republic of Korea.

5. Renee will not eat chicken because she has chicken for the pet.

6. Jenny had always wanted to work in the large company, but a company she wanted to work in would not hire her, so she joined small company instead.

7. White House is official residence for president of United States.

8. Homeless in Seoul often find shelter in a Seoul Station on cold nights.

9. Kennedys live on the St. Denis street which is located the north of St. Laurent street.

10. Chinese in the Taiwan speak Mandarin, and Chinese in Guangdong province speak Cantonese.

11. He wants to eat *kimchi*; however, *kimchi* in his refrigerator is now rotten.

12. June does not like the *ddeok*, but she ate piece of *ddeok* because it was served at her friend's wedding.

13. I would give you piece of paper, but there is no the paper left.

Activity 2

After reading the following passages, fill in the missing articles.

Yeon Hee has violin that costs over million dollars because she is professional violinist. She has been playing violin since she was three years old, and she won first prize in her second competition when she was only four. At age seven, she was accepted into prestigious Seoul Performing Arts Academy and quickly progressed to senior position in youth orchestra. Later, Yeon Hee moved to London when she was 15 years old to pursue her dream of becoming professional violinist. These days Yeon Hee regularly plays with London Symphony Orchestra, but she has yet to be asked to be soloist.

Great Lakes are five lakes located along Canadian-American border. While each lake is a separate body of water, they are connected through rivers and canals. For instance, Niagara River connects Lake Huron to Lake Ontario at the city of Niagara Falls, and Welland Canal connects Lake Erie and Lake Ontario. Saint Lawrence River takes the water from all of these lakes to Atlantic Ocean by way of Quebec and Gaspé Peninsula. Water in these lakes provides water and power to many important North American cities surrounding lakes including Chicago, Detroit, and Toronto.

2 Capitalization

When English letters are written in their uppercase form, the process is called "capitalization." The following chart shows when letters are usually capitalized.

Use	Examples
The first word of a sentence	Exchange programs provide students with many benefits.
"I"	When I was in high school, I studied until midnight every night.
Every word in a title (except articles, prepositions, and coordinating conjunctions unless they appear at the beginning of a title)	*The Wind in the Willows*
Proper nouns (Specific or unique nouns)	
• Organizations	• the World Health Organization.
• Places	• Sungkyunkwan University is an old university.
• Brands	• Starbucks Coffee Company has good coffee.
• Geographical regions	• There are many conflicts in the Middle East.
• Names, titles, names before titles, titles before names	• Professor Lee is a famous professor. • Aunt Sarah is my favorite aunt.
• Days, months, holidays	• In 2011, Children's Day, which is always on May 5th, fell on a Thursday.
Words derived from proper nouns (adjectives, languages, etc)	Spanish is spoken in Spain by Spaniards.
Course titles	Because he was a biology major, he took Introduction to Biology.

Grammar Tip

Capitalization and Names

Some names have unique capitalization rules because of their origin.

Jane McNeil   Charles de Gaulle   Vincent van Gogh

Korean names are generally capitalized in one of four ways.

Young Sang Lee   Young-Sang Lee   Youngsang Lee   Lee Youngsang

Some people choose to write their given name as Yeongsang, which conforms to the South Korean government's standard system.

The South Korean government's standard system can be found at https://www.korean.go.kr/front_eng/roman/roman_01.do

Activity 1

Read the following sentences, and highlight the words which should be capitalized.

1. before i went to portugal last year, i studied portuguese.

2. sam failed history 101 last year because history is his worst subject.

3. professor lee asked john if he had finished reading jane austen's *pride and prejudice*.

4. there is a mr. pizza pizza restaurant located very close to hyehwa station.

5. when korean thanksgiving falls on a tuesday or thursday, it is a five day holiday, but when it falls on a saturday, sunday, or wednesday, it is only a three day holiday.

6. there are many ways to experience nature in seoul: bukhan mountain, the han river, and the cheonggye stream.

7. after watching the movie *the devil wears prada*, jenny decided to go to new york city instead of visiting europe.

8. there is about 1,050mg of sodium in a serving of shin ramyun which is surprisingly more sodium than the 1,010 mg found in a mcdonald's big mac.

9. lee hyo ri's song "chitty chitty bang bang" has nothing to do with ian fleming's 1964 novel by the same name.

10. professor webster is a south african anthropologist who is best known for his contribution to the anti–apartheid movement.

Activity 2

Read the following passages and highlight the letters which should be capitalized.

shanghai, in the people's republic of china, is a fabulous city to visit. tourists who love sports can visit during the chinese grand prix or watch the city's basketball team, the shanghai sharks play. for those who prefer to spend their time in museums, the shanghai art museum in people's square houses a large number of exhibitions. at night, the bund is a fantastic area to see historic buildings and view architecturally interesting buildings such as the oriental pearl tower across the huangpu river. therefore, there are many diverse places to visit and sites to see in shanghai.

ban ki-moon has had an interesting life. he was born in a small village in north chungcheong province, but in 1962, he won a red cross essay contest which allowed him to move to san francisco where he was able to improve his english skills. during his time in the united states of america, he met president john f. kennedy. after attending seoul national university and harvard university, he became a diplomat and later, the head of the ministry of foreign affairs and trade in south korea. he presently holds the position of secretary general at the united nations. thus, his life is an inspiration for younger koreans who want to serve their country on an international level.

Prepositions

» Prepositions of Time

The following prepositions are commonly used to discuss time.

Preposition	Use	Examples
At	Precise times	Class begins at 9 am. We take a break at dinnertime.
In	General times • months, years, centuries, long periods	He was born in July in 1980. Sungkyunkwan University was founded in the 14th century. We have class in the morning.
On	Specific times • dates and days	His birthday is on July 31. On White Day, men give women candy.
During	Development through a period	During the month of July, there is often a lot of rain. During the Seollal period, there are no classes.
For	Length of time	We have been in class for twenty minutes.
Since	Beginning of a period	We have been in class since 9 am.
Until	Continuance until a specific time	You will have until the end of class to finish the exam. Students have until December 1st to hand in their papers.
From-To	A specific time period	You will have from 9 am to 10:15 am to finish the exam.

» Prepositions of Location

The following prepositions are often used to discuss the location of a person or object.

Preposition	Use	Examples
At	General spaces Paper Groups of people	At the bus stop, at the movie theater At the top/bottom of the page At the front/back of the class
In	Spaces with boundaries Bodies of water Lines	I am watching a movie in the theater. In the sea In a row/in a line
On	Surfaces Small islands Directions	On the wall/table On Maui On the left/right

Irregular Examples

Travel: on foot   in taxis/cars   on bikes/boats/public transportation
Corner: in a room corner   at/on a street corner

» Prepositions of Space

The following are common prepositions to explain where an object or a person is located.

Above	Around	Beyond	Near	Through
Across	Behind	By	Nearby	Toward
Against	Below	Down	Next to	Under
Ahead of	Beneath	From	On top of	Underneath
Along	Beside	In front of	Outside (of)	Up
Among	Between	Inside	Over	Within

Students need to also be aware of how prepositions are used with media.

The song was on the radio.   He listens to the radio every day.
I saw a program on television.   I read the article on the Internet.
I read the essay in a book/newspaper/magazine.

Activity 1

Complete the following sentences.

1. Are your children _____ the festival?

2. There is a beautiful picture _____ the wall.

3. I am _____ school, _____ the classroom, _____ the fourth floor.

4. _____ as long as I can remember, that elderly man has lived _____ that house _____ the corner of the street.

5. I missed my favorite program _____ television because I was reading a very exciting part _____ my book, so I had to watch the show later _____ the Internet.

Activity 2

Read the following sentences and insert the appropriate prepositions where necessary.

1. Jane is arriving January 26th 2 o'clock the afternoon.

2. It snows here every year December, so we always go outside and play the snow Christmas Day.

3. Michael came here foot, but because of the flood, he had to leave a boat.

4. Frankie started working for her law firm 1995.

5. Jill began working on the project yesterday.

6. 2003, the students have eaten the cafeteria lunchtime. However, before there was a cafeteria, the students usually ate the large leafy trees.

7. When the taxis are a line, you have to take the taxi the others.

8. The students the back of the class should write their names the top of the page.

9. At the moment, he is Jeju Island, but because he is afraid of fish the water, he is spending all of his time his hotel swimming pool.

10. You have 10 am 11 am to complete the exam. Please write all of the information the box provided. Please also remember to keep your eyes the paper, and do not look at the papers of the students sitting you.

11. Over a year, a burglar has been breaking into buildings late night and stealing jewelry from locked cases. One night, a police officer heard a noise and went to investigate. The burglar heard him, so he jumped out of a window and into a truck. However, the police officer saw the numbers the license plate and was able to catch the criminal.

4 Conditionals

Conditionals are used to show cause and effect relationships. They are complex sentences which consist of an "if" (sometimes "when") subordinating clause and a "main" independent clause.

Type	Construction	Examples
Type 0 Usual, habitual, or scientific fact	**If/When**: present simple **Main**: present simple	When I come to school, I take the bus. If I drink tea, I drink green tea. When water reaches 71 degrees at the top of Mt. Everest, it boils.
Type 1 Possible, likely to happen in the near future	**If**: present simple **Main**: will + base verb	If the weather is warm, we will go swimming. If I have an "A" average, I will get a scholarship. If the situation continues, profits will decrease.
Type 2 Unreal, unlikely to happen in the present	**If**: past simple **Main**: would*** + base verb	If aliens attacked, I would fight them. If I were you, I would not do that. If I saw a burglary, I would call the police.
Type 3 Impossible past, regrets, imagining a different reality based on a different past	**If**: past perfect **Main**: would have + past participle	If aliens had attacked, I would have fought them. If I had been you, I would not have done that. If I had seen a burglary, I would have called the police.

***In Type 2 or 3 conditionals, "would" can be replaced with "might" (possibility) or "could" (option/ability).

> 💡 **Grammar Tip**
>
> In some cases, more than one type can be used to show different meanings.
>
> **Examples**:
> If I become the President, I will lower taxes. (a candidate in an election)
> If I became the President, I would lower taxes. (regular people)
>
> If our team wins, we will all cheer. (optimistic)
> If our team won, we would all cheer. (pessimistic)

Grammar Tip

Second Conditional

When using the second conditional in the first person, use "were" instead of "was."
Example: If I were you, I would apply for the position.

Activity 1

Identify the following conditionals, and answer the questions.

1. When you exercise, what kind of exercise do you do? Type: 0 / 1 / 2 / 3

   When I exercise, I play basketball.

2. If you were a horse, how would your life be different? Type: 0 / 1 / 2 / 3

3. If there is Asian dust tomorrow, will you go hiking? Type: 0 / 1 / 2 / 3

4. If you moved to another country, where would you want to live? Type: 0 / 1 / 2 / 3

5. If you get a job this vacation, what kind of work will you do? Type: 0 / 1 / 2 / 3

6. When you feel sad, how do you make yourself feel happy again? Type: 0 / 1 / 2 / 3

7. If you meet your friends this weekend, where will you go? Type: 0 / 1 / 2 / 3

8. If you saw a murder being committed, what would you do? Type: 0 / 1 / 2 / 3

9. If North Korea had won the Korean War, how would life have been different?
   Type: 0 / 1 / 2 / 3

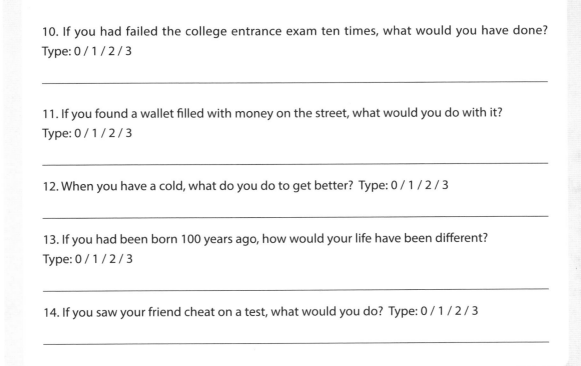

10. If you had failed the college entrance exam ten times, what would you have done?
Type: 0 / 1 / 2 / 3

_____

11. If you found a wallet filled with money on the street, what would you do with it?
Type: 0 / 1 / 2 / 3

_____

12. When you have a cold, what do you do to get better? Type: 0 / 1 / 2 / 3

_____

13. If you had been born 100 years ago, how would your life have been different?
Type: 0 / 1 / 2 / 3

_____

14. If you saw your friend cheat on a test, what would you do? Type: 0 / 1 / 2 / 3

_____

Activity 2

On a separate piece of paper, make your own Type 0–3 conditionals for another classmate to answer.

Activity 3

Choose one of the topics from Activity 1, and write a paragraph on the topic.

5 Modals

Modal verbs modify other verbs to show permission, ability, possibility, and obligation.

» Permission/Request

Can	Informal – question	Can I have some water?
May	Formal – question	May I borrow your pen?
Could	Formal – question	Could I use your phone?
Would	Formal/polite – question or statement	Would you like a drink? I would like a glass of water.

» Ability

Can/cannot	Present ability	He can ski. He cannot surf.
Could/could not	Past ability Option – polite or ability	He could ski when he was young. We could ski, or we could snowboard.

» Possibility

May/may not	Moderate future possibility	The bus may be here in five minutes.
Might/might not	Moderate present possibility Moderate future possibility	The bus might be here soon. The bus might be here in five minutes.
Should/should not	Stronger possibility	The bus should be here soon.
Must/must not	Certainty	The bus must be here by now.
Will/will not	Future certainty	The bus will arrive at 9 pm.

» Suggestions/Obligation

Should/should not	Recommendation Duty (Can be refused)	You should eat at that new restaurant. I should go to the party, but I am sick.
Ought to / ought not to	Necessity (ethical)	Leaders ought to set a good example.
Must	Necessity (personal feeling)	I must study harder if I want to pass.
Must not	Negative law	Passengers must not bring guns on planes.
Have to *** (Need to)	Necessity (from an outside source - parents, teachers, boss, law, reason)	My teacher said I have to study harder. I have to write a quiz today. Korean drivers have to wear seatbelts.
Do not have to ***	Not necessary	Cyclists do not have to wear a helmet.
(Had) better (not) ***	Warning	You better write the quiz, or you will fail. You better not swim in shark infested water.

***These phrases are not modal verbs, but they are often used in a similar way as modal verbs.

Activity 1

Fill in the blanks with the appropriate word(s).

Hyun Gee has a weight problem. He knows that he _____ eat fresh fruits and vegetables instead of instant or fatty food, and he _____ eat healthy food because he lives in the countryside; however, he prefers to eat junk food every day. Because his father died early from a heart attack, he has always known that he _____ have heart problems in the future. However, yesterday he went to the doctor who told him that he _____ start eating better because his health is in serious trouble. In fact, the doctor said that he _____ lose weight immediately, and he _____ eat any more fast food, or he _____ have a heart attack within the next few months. Needless to say, now Hyun Gee knows how serious the situation is, he also feels that he _____ lose weight.

When Ga Eun started her job, she was told that she _____ work overtime unless she wanted to do extra work. She was also told that she _____ be able to get a promotion within six months like more than two thirds of her other coworkers. However, she now realizes that if her boss asks her if she _____ work overtime, it really means that she _____ work late regardless of whether or not she has other plans. She now also knows that she _____ never complain about her work hours because then she most certainly _____ get a promotion.

Waiter: "Good evening, Sir. _____ I take your order?"

Customer: "Yes, I _____ like to order red wine and steak with a side order of salad."

W: "I'm sorry, Sir, but tonight we _____ serve that dish because we are out of steak. You _____ order grilled chicken, or you _____ have oysters instead."

C: "Unfortunately, I _____ eat oysters because I'm allergic to them, so I guess I _____ order the grilled chicken."

W: "_____ you like to order dessert now?"

C: "I _____ have dessert later, but I'm not sure yet."

W: "Very well, Sir. I _____ be back in a moment with your wine."

Activity 2

Using the modal verb and conditional lessons, answer the questions in full conditional sentences.

Example: Hyun Young got lost driving to the beach. What could she have done to have avoided getting lost?

Possible Answer: If I had been Hyun Young, I would have used my GPS.

1. Hyun Seok lost a million won gambling at the casino. What could he have done with that money?

_____

2. A business owner needs to cut costs. What usually happens in this situation?

_____

3. Elizabeth did not like her new boss, so she quit her job immediately. Are there any other ways she might have solved her problem?

_____

4. Hwa Kyung just found a diamond ring on the street. If you were her, what would you do?

_____

5. A student went out drinking the night before his exam. What usually happens in this situation?

_____

6. Seung Ho is watching two teenagers beat up a homeless man. If you were him, what would you do?

_____

7. Min Kyoung has a blind date tomorrow. What do you think might happen?

_____

8. A twelve-year-old boy runs away from home. What might happen to him?

_____

9. Young Jun forgot to lock the door when he left home. What could happen to his house?

_____

6 Adjectives

Adjectives are descriptive words which modify or give more details about nouns.

Example: I have a car.

Example: I have a shiny new black car.

In the above example, the adjectives are in front of the noun; however, adjectives can follow nouns if you use sense verbs (smell, taste, look, etc.) or verbs of being (be, seem).

Example: The car looked shiny and new.

💡 Grammar Tip

As in most English grammar rules, there are some exceptions to adjective order, most notably, words, titles, or phrases which have been influenced by French.

Example: Boutros Boutros Ghali is a former Secretary General of the United Nations.

» Adjective Order

When using more than one adjective, it is important to know the order in which they should be placed.

Determiner	Characteristic	Physical Description				Origin	Material	Qualifier
		Size	Shape	Age	Color			
three	funny	big	flat	old	red	Kenyan	wood	baseball
a	shiny	small	square	new	blue	Western	gold	computer
some	sweet	tiny	round	one year old	pink	British	glass	sports
many	terrifying	huge	spherical	vintage	white	Cartier	leather	homemade

---

💡 Grammar Tip

In general, writers should not use more than three adjectives (not including the determiner) in a row to describe a noun.

Examples: Three funny old baseball players were teaching children how to play the game.
A shiny new gold watch was lying on the ground.
Some sweet British grandmothers raised money to help homeless dogs.
Many terrifying huge white dogs attacked me.

186

Grammar Tip

If there are two adjectives of the same type, the order does not matter, but they should be separated by a comma.

Example: The crunchy, sweet cookies were homemade.
Example: The sweet, crunchy cookies were homemade.

Activity 1

Identify the adjectives in the sentence and their type. Then correct the sentence if it is in the wrong order.

1. The actress famous lived in a brick modest simple home.

_____

2. Yoon Jin's loud annoying parrot lives in a black metal enormous cage.

_____

3. Paul told his friends about the ferocious puppy Dalmatian.

_____

4. The ancient German castle sat empty in the open field.

_____

5. Donna brought back silk from India flowing soft.

_____

6. A black ugly old cat scared me when it jumped from the window to the ground.

_____

7. I could not study because there were noisy four women laughing loudly.

_____

8. Ainsley's fiancé gave her a ring diamond expensive Tiffany.

_____

9. These kiwis green New Zealand are both tangy and sweet.

_____

10. The students journalism decided to start new campus a newspaper.

_____

» Adjective Clauses

Adjective clauses are dependent clauses which modify nouns to give more information or to clarify a noun.

Example: Blizzards are dangerous storms which include high winds and heavy snowfall.

Relative Pronouns

Adjective clauses always require relative pronouns. The following chart organizes the type of relative pronoun, and its place or function in a sentence.

Function	People	Things	Place	Time	Explanation
Subject	Who, that	Which, that			
Object	That, whom	Which, that	Where, which	when	What, why
Possessive	Whose	Whose, of which			

Example:

Is that the person who stole your wallet? (subject)

Is that the person whom you mugged? (object)

Is that the person whose wallet was stolen? (possessive)

💡 Grammar Tip

When talking about a place, "which" is more formal than "where," and "whom" is generally more formal than "that" in English sentences.

Example: "There is the place where she met her husband." (informal)
Example: "There is the place at which she met her husband" (formal)

Similarly, "that" is more often used in informal English than "who" (for people) or "which" (for things). However, "that" is the preferred relative pronoun in two cases.

1. Indefinite pronouns
Example: I told him to pack **everything** that fits in the suitcases.

2. Nouns modified by superlatives
Example: He is **the fastest** runner that the world has ever seen.

Types of Adjective Clauses

There are two types of adjective clauses, the restrictive relative clause and the non-restrictive relative clause.

Restrictive Relative Clause

Example: A farmer is a person who grows crops and raises livestock.

Non-Restrictive Relative Clause

Example: Julie's farm, which had been owned by her family for a century, was sold last week.

 Grammar Tip

Commas are not usually used after the relative pronoun in the defining relative clause. However, if additional information is given in the non-defining relative clause that is not necessary to understand the meaning of the subject of the sentence, then commas are necessary.

My sister, who lives in Ireland, is studying medicine. (one sister)
My sister who lives in Ireland is a student. My sister who lives in Hong Kong is a business person.

Activity 1

Choose the correct relative pronoun for formal writing.

1. Is Lisa the girl _____ dress was ruined?

2. Do you know the actor _____ is the villain in this movie?

3. Eun Joo, _____ was falsely accused of murder, spent ten years
   in the jail _____ is located just outside of the city.

4. Is she the one _____ you are going to invite to the party?

5. He is the youngest chef _____ has ever graduated from this cooking academy.

6. Do you know the reason _____ so few people came to this event?

7. George has a car _____ is always breaking down, but he can take it to his uncle's
   repair shop _____ is cheaper than other places.

Activity 2

Add commas to the following sentences where appropriate.

1. Glenn is a boy who loves horses.

2. They hired the quiet woman whom the boss interviewed last week.

3. The company which is located on the other side of the street has 532 employees.

4. Gregor's Hamburgers which is the largest restaurant chain in the city was established in 1962.

5. The man whose leg was hurt in a car accident was taken to the hospital by ambulance.

6. Where is the good looking guy whom you want to invite to the party?

7. Robson Motors which is the top ranking car company in the country had to recall thousands of cars last week because of engine problems.

8. The textbook which is on top of Yong Hee's desk is the textbook for this class.

9. *Gray's Anatomy* which has been an extremely important medical textbook for the past 150 years was written by Henry Gray.

10. The house which is located at the end of the street is mine.

Activity 3

Write your own definitions for the following nouns using adjective clauses.

1. Bees

_____

2. Mothers

_____

3. Passports

_____

4. Love

_____

5. Education

_____

Active vs. Passive Voice

One of the first lessons students learn when they begin to study English sentence structure is English sentences are usually ordered this way: subject + verb + object. The subject performs the action, the verb is the action, and the object is the recipient of the action.

> subject   object
> **Example**: The **cat ate** the **mouse**.
> verb

This sentence structure is called "active voice," and it is the preferred order for many kinds of writing, especially in the humanities. Nevertheless, a different kind of sentence structure called "passive voice" is also necessary in certain instances.

> **Example**: The mouse was eaten by the cat.
> auxiliary verb (form of "to be") + main verb (past participle) + (by) = passive voice

The above example, the object and subject switch places without changing the underlying meaning of the sentence.

Passive use is the preferable form of sentence structure in the following instances:

Situation	Explanation	Example
Scientific reports and papers	Passive voice is considered more objective in science.	Cancerous cells were found in the samples.
Emphasizing an object	Sometimes emphasizing the object is more dramatic, or authors want to emphasize the effect instead of the cause.	Millions of people were killed by the government during the bloody conflict.
Uncertain, unclear, or unknown subject	In some cases, the subject is either unknown or unimportant in the sentence.	The windows were broken around midnight.

🔍 Grammar Tip

The auxiliary verb (to be) changes depending on the time period and amount.

The prisoner **was brought** yesterday.
The prisoners **are being brought** in at this moment.
The prisoner **will be brought** in tomorrow.

Activity 1

Change the following active sentences into passive sentences.

1. Most Koreans eat *kimchi*.

   _____

2. Heavy rain caused a landslide.

   _____

3. A massive earthquake and tsunami damaged the Fukushima Daiichi nuclear plant in 2011.

   _____

4. Sir Edmund Hillary and Tenzing Norgay were the first people to successfully reach the summit of Mt. Everest in 1953.

   _____

5. Kim Yuna won the gold medal in women's figure skating at the 2010 Winter Olympic Games.

   _____

Activity 2

Change the following passive sentences into active sentences. If there is no clear actor in the original sentence, use common sense to determine the subject in the active sentence.

1. He was hired for the new position.

   _____

2. The bathrooms are cleaned at around 1 pm.

   _____

3. The student was failed for plagiarizing her essay.

   _____

4. Hangul was developed in the 15th century.

   _____

5. English is taught in this class.

   _____

6. Lee Myung-bak was elected as the President of the Republic of Korea in 2008.

   _____

8 Comparatives and Superlatives

Writers often use adjectives or descriptive words to describe the nouns they are using. Sometimes when there is more than one noun, writers want to talk about differences between the nouns by using comparatives and superlatives.

Comparatives compare two adjectives describing nouns while superlatives show the greatest degree of a characteristic.

Examples:
This dress is more expensive than that dress. (comparative)
This dress is the most expensive in the store. (superlative)

» Adjective Modification

Adjectives are modified as comparatives and superlatives based on the number of syllables or beats in the word.

Examples:
Beautiful - Beau/ti/ful (3 syllables)
More/less beautiful (comparative)
The most/the least beautiful (superlative)

Sweet (1 syllable)
Sweeter (comparative)
Sweetest (superlative)

Learners should note that their first language often affects their second, and this can lead to an atypical number of syllables. For example, Korean speakers often pronounce *cute* (one syllable) as *kju-teu* (two syllables). Learners are therefore advised to familiarize themselves with typical pronunciation before modifying adjectives.

Example:
Cute: Cute (English - 1 syllable) verses Cue/tuh (Korean - 2 syllable)

Therefore, students need to make sure they are sounding out syllables with English pronunciation before they modify adjectives.

» Constructing Comparatives and Superlatives

Rule	Comparative Form	Superlative Form
1 syllable ending in "e" fine, wide	Add "r" finer, wider	Add "st" finest, widest
1 syllable ending in 1 vowel and 1 consonant hot, sad	Double the consonant + "er" hotter, sadder	Double the consonant +est hottest, saddest
1 syllable ending in more than 1 consonant or vowel strange, cool	Add + "er" stranger, cooler	Add "est" strangest, coolest
2 syllables ending in "y" silly, funny	"y" ⇨ "i" + "er" sillier, funnier	"y" ⇨ "i" + "est" silliest, funniest
2 syllables or more (not ending in "y") beautiful, expensive	Add "more" more beautiful, more expensive	Add "most" most beautiful, most expensive

Word	Comparative Form	Superlative form
clever	cleverer/more clever	cleverest/most clever
gentle	gentler/more gentle	gentlest/most gentle
friendly	friendlier/more friendly	friendliest/most friendly
quiet	quieter/ more quiet	quietest/most quiet
simple	simpler/more simple	simplest/most simple

The following adjectives are irregular and do not follow the previously given rules.

Word	Comparative Form	Superlative Form
good	better	best
bad	worse	worst
far	farther	farthest
little	less	least
many	more	most

Signpost See page 170 for information about the definite article and superlatives.

Activity 1

Read the following passages and modify them as appropriate.

At first glance, it does not seem that Hyea Su is a unique student. She is smart, but there are other students who are smart than her. Similarly, when playing sports, she is not the fast or the slow student, and half of the class can run far than her in little time than she can run. However, Hyea Su is a very funny girl, and she tells the good jokes and stories her friends have ever heard. Her classmates think that one day she may become famous comedian in Korea because of her great sense of humor.

Andy wanted to buy a new car. He was not looking for the cheap car or the expensive car but for a mid-priced vehicle. Initially, the car salesperson showed him a red car and a black car. The red car accelerated fast and had good features than the black car, but the black car was many fuel efficient and had a sleek design than the other car. Andy could not decide which car was good. Finally, the salesperson showed him a white car. It was a bit expensive than the other two, but in every other way, it was the good of the three cars. In the end, Andy drove home happy in his brand new white car.

9 Using Non-English Words in English

What Is the Difference Between a Sundae and *Sundae*?

Using italics helps the reader to understand the difference between an English term and a word from another language. Using Korean, Chinese, or words from any other language is perfectly acceptable in English assignments as long as the word is written and explained properly.

Step 1: Romanize the word.

Words written in other scripts need to be written in Roman characters.

비빔밥 → bibimbap

月饼 → yue bing

Step 2: Italics and capitalization

Non-English general nouns need to be italicized and left in lower case letters if they have not been accepted into the English language.

bibimbap → *bibimbap*

yue bing → *yue bing*

> **Signpost** See page 173 for more information on proper and general nouns.

If these words are written by hand, they should be underlined.

bibimbap → <u>bibimbap</u>

Proper nouns should not be italicized, and the first letter of each word should be capitalized.

Seoul → Seoul

kim eun jee → Kim Eun Jee

Step 3: Define and incorporate into a sentence

Writers should never assume their readers know non-English words; therefore, general nouns need to be explained or defined the first time they are used. Non English words should also conform to English grammar rules.

Bibimbap is a Korean dish that consists of mixed rice, vegetables, egg, and red pepper paste.

Yue bing is a traditional Chinese dessert that is eaten during the Mid-Autumn Festival.

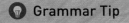 Grammar Tip

If a non-English word has an easy translation, use the appropriate English word.

She wore a beautiful *jinju* necklace. → She wore a beautiful pearl necklace.

Activity 1

Change the following words into Roman script and decide if these words should be italicized (underlined) or capitalized.

막걸리	고추장	고시원	김치찌개
삼겹살	설날	호떡	대구시
대구	성균관대학교	上海	餃子

Activity 2

Now use simple adjective clauses to define these words in a sentence.

막걸리 _____

고추장 _____

삼겹살 _____

김치찌개 _____

호떡 _____

설날 _____

餃子 _____

Signpost See page 188 for more information on simple adjective clauses.

Activity 3

Using the space provided, rewrite one of the following paragraphs using the steps previously covered.

추석 is a wonderful way to experience unique aspects of Korean culture. For instance, food is a very important part of the holiday. For dinner, Koreans usually eat 불고기 and 잡채. They also eat 송편 or drink 식혜 after the main meal. Many families also engage in tradition when they perform 차례 by a special table set with offerings of food such as 밥, 과일, and 생선. Sometimes families will even dress in 한복 for this activity. Finally, some Koreans still enjoy watching 씨름 matches during the vacation period. Thus, 추석 is a great way to understand traditional Korean culture.

北京 is a great place to travel on vacation. First, 毛澤東's tomb is an important place to visit to understand the history of China, and 万里长城 is located close to the city, allowing visitors to visit it easily. In addition, many kinds of food are found throughout the city. 北京烤鸭 is the most famous. However, 烙饼 is also a quick snack tourists can enjoy. Finally, no trip is complete without a trip to the 京剧. Therefore, if tourists want a fun-filled destination where they can eat local delicacies, they should visit 北京.

Academic Writing Techniques

Do not use the following writing techniques when writing academic or formal assignments.

Problem	Correction
Coordinating Conjunctions • Do not use to begin a sentence.	~~So~~ this method is effective. Thus, this method is effective.
Abbreviations	~~TV~~ -Television
Acronyms • The first time, write out the full term before putting the acronym in brackets, and use only the acronym afterwards.	Post-Traumatic Stress Disorder (PTSD)
Truncations	~~Sat.~~ – Saturday
Contractions	~~Won't~~ – Will not
Emoticons and Text Language	~~*^_^*~~
Singular Nouns • Replace with plural nouns when talking about general characteristics or norms.	~~An apple is crunchier than an orange.~~ Apples are crunchier than oranges.
Gender Exclusive Language • Do not use pronouns, terms, or expressions which exclude a gender.	~~Fireman~~-Firefighter ~~If a person is sick, he should go to a hospital.~~ If people are sick, they should go to a hospital.
Etc./and so on/… (unfinished sentences)	~~Carrots, cucumbers etc. have many vitamins.~~ Vegetables such as carrots or cucumbers have many vitamins.
Regional English varieties such as Korean and Chinese English	~~I have a promise tonight.~~ I have plans/an appointment tonight.

Numbers

The writing rules for numbers vary depending on style guide and situation, but writers often follow these guidelines. Overall, be consistent, and check with your professor for discipline-specific rules.

Figures • Numbers that take more than two words to spell out, specific numbers	1984, 152 elephants, 2%, $5.56, page 42, 8.3 kilometers, 17 Millard Street
Numbers in Full • Numbers at the beginning of sentences, numbers that take two or fewer words to spell, rounded numbers	One elephant, twenty-two officials, millions of people

Activity 1

Rewrite the following sentences to correct the inappropriate academic language.

1. SKKU was the first uni in Korea when it opened in thirteen ninety eight. At first, SKKU focused on teaching material related only to Confucianism, but now students can study film, Russian, engineering, etc.

_____

_____

2. Jan. 1st is a public holiday in Korea. But because the lunar calendar is also used, Seollal, or Lunar New Year's Day, is also celebrated in Jan. or Feb.

_____

_____

3. If a student is late for the quiz, test, exam and so on, he will not be allowed extra time. And he will also lose participation marks because he was not in class for the full time.

_____

_____

4. Many young people can't find full time employment in part because last month the unemployment rate rose to four point four percent which is a 9 year high.

_____

_____

5. MADD (Mothers Against Drunk Driving) is an organization that educates people about the dangers of driving cars, trucks, boats etc. while impaired.

_____

_____

6. The Korean Air flight leaves at eleven forty-five am, but passengers shouldn't be late because they need to be at their gate 1 hour before boarding.

_____

_____

Using Certain Pronouns

When writing high-level academic papers, it is sometimes appropriate for advanced students to use personal pronouns. However, academic writing usually requires objective language that is distanced from the author's direct personal opinion, and when learning how to write, students should try to avoid:

I/Me/My/Mine	Direct personal opinion should be replaced with research or logical arguments.	~~I think this cancer drug is effective.~~ Research shows this cancer drug is effective.
You/Your/Yours	In some cases, using "you" may be inappropriate or offensive to the audience.	~~You should exercise to control your weight.~~ People should exercise to control their weight.
We/Our/Ours	Academic writing should be used to communicate to a wider audience, not just to your particular group.	~~In our culture, we eat kimchi.~~ In Korea, the locals eat kimchi.
I/We vs. You Us. vs. Them	Try to avoid language which unnecessarily polarizes groups.	~~We have different views than them.~~ Students have different views than teachers.

Activity 2

Rewrite the following sentences without using personal pronouns.

1. You should be more concerned with climate change and the state of our planet.

   _____

   _____

2. We all know that unemployment is a problem in our country.

   _____

   _____

3. I think Korea is a safe country because I feel safe walking around late at night.

   _____

   _____

4. In my opinion, migration is one of the biggest issues of our time.

   _____

   _____

Academic Register

In English, there are four general registers: high formal, formal, informal, and familiar. Each register has a place in speaking and writing, but students need to understand the differences between them and use them appropriately. Academic writing tends to take the formal register, but students may encounter other registers when reading research and texts.

High Formal

This register is common in very formal speeches, and students will read it in historical documents. However, students need to avoid writing in this register as it does not suit academic writing.

Example: "We the people of Korea, proud of a resplendent history and traditions dating from time immemorial, upholding the cause of the Provisional Republic of Korea Government born of the March First Independence Movement of 1919…" ("Preamble" of The Constitution of the Republic of Korea).

Formal

This register uses more objective and precise language than lower formal speech, and it is more accessible than language used in the higher register.

Example: The Constitution of the Republic of Korea commences by contextualizing the document in Korea's historic struggle for independence.

Informal

Informal register is often used in journalism and other popular forms of writing. It tends to use a more casual and conversational tone and more colloquial language while still retaining a more formal tone than the familiar register.

Example: The Constitution begins by talking about Korea's long fight for independence.

Familiar

The lowest register is used between people who are very close to each other in casual settings or on social media or in personal correspondence where formal vocabulary and sentence structure would sound too distant or official.

Example: On #constitutionday let's remember our fight for freedom!

Transitioning from Informal to Formal Academic Writing

Sometimes vocabulary needs to be changed to make the sentence more formal and appropriate for an academic setting.

Informal: The politician was <u>thrown out</u> of Congress for acting <u>crazy.</u>
Formal: The politician was <u>ejected from</u> Congress for acting <u>erratically</u>.

Sometimes vocabulary and sentence structure need to be changed at the same time to sound more appropriate for academic writing.

Informal: If the minimum wage increases, businesses <u>are gonna say it is okay to raise prices.</u>
Formal: If the minimum wage increases, businesses <u>will contend that price increases are acceptable.</u>

Activity 3

Read the following sentences, and change the underlined words into vocabulary from the formal register. However, avoid using language which is high formal.

The official ~~took back~~ his statement. - Informal
The official **retracted** his statement. - Formal
The official ~~abjured~~ his statement. - High Formal

1. Queen Victoria's <u>mom</u> raised her in a strict system of rules called the Kensington System.

_____

2. Airlines need to improve the way they <u>check</u> passenger identification.

_____

3. The workers <u>got fired.</u>

_____

4. There's <u>gonna be big</u> consequences for the economy if these trends continue.

_____

5. Many university students <u>rack up</u> enormous student loans to <u>pay for</u> their education.

_____

6. The <u>kids</u> <u>said sorry</u> for causing the damage.

_____

7. Students who are <u>lucky</u> enough to study essay writing in high school are likely to <u>get</u> higher grades in university classes.

_____

8. The president was <u>lost for words</u> when she <u>looked at</u> the destruction caused by the typhoon.

_____

9. Customers can be <u>talked into buying more stuff.</u>

_____

10. The students <u>wanna re-write the exam because they got lots of wrong answers.</u>

_____

Simple and Direct Questions

In higher level writing, questions are used in a variety of ways, but when students begin writing, they often misuse them. Writers need to avoid asking simple questions or posing direct questions.

Asking the reader direct questions • The reader cannot respond to your question while reading.	Why do you think junk food is harmful?
Answering simple questions immediately after asking them • It is better to concisely prove your argument with evidence.	Is junk food unhealthy? Yes it is.
Giving an answer as an incomplete sentence	Is junk food unhealthy? Yes.

The questions above can be rephrased as more substantive statements to make a better impact in academic writing.

Give your reader answers instead of posing direct questions.	~~Why do you think junk food is harmful?~~ Junk food is harmful because it contains an excess of calories and fat.
State your position clearly in a full sentence.	~~Is junk food unhealthy? Yes.~~ Junk food is unhealthy for a number of reasons. Junk food is unhealthy because it contributes to heart disease and diabetes.

Activity 3

Re-write the following questions into a substantive sentence.

1. Why should people stop smoking?

_____

2. Are there any benefits to living on a farm? Yes.

_____

3. Why is there climate change?

_____

Professional Writing Techniques

Professional writing techniques builds upon academic writing techniques and is used to convey information efficiently and effectively such as reports in the scientific and business domains.

What Makes Effective Professional Writing?

1. It is simple – Avoid using complicated words when simpler words will suffice. Use jargon only when necessary.

> **Good example:**
> Researchers should be **aware** of the limitations of their study.
>
> **Poor example:**
> Researchers should be **cognizant** of the limitations of their study.
>
> ~~facilitate~~ – help
> ~~initiate~~ – start
> ~~extensive~~ – common
> ~~ornate~~ – fancy
> ~~crux~~ – main point
> ~~salient~~ – common / important

2. It is clear – Define terms and technical language.

> **Good example:**
> Recession is defined in several ways: shrinking gross domestic product over six months or a 1.5 to 2 % increase in unemployment over one year.
>
> **Poor example:**
> Recession is bad for the economy.

3. It uses active voice – Active voice helps provide clarity as it focuses on the subject. However, sometimes passive voice must be used to avoid first person or to emphasize the object.

> **Good example:**
> Johnson theorized the presence of parents influenced their children's behavior.
>
> **Poor example:**
> It was theorized that the children's behavior was influenced by the presence of their parents.

> **Signpost** See page 191 for more information about active and passive voice.

4. It is impartial – Avoid making assumptions or using emotional language.

> **Good example:**
> Three participants were excluded because they incorrectly filled out the survey.
>
> **Poor example:**
> It is unfortunate that some of the participants filled out survey incorrectly. Because of this, we had to exclude three participants from the study.

5. It is concise and precise – avoid making assumptions or using emotional language

Problem	Correction
Redundant Words	~~At this present time~~ – Now ~~conducted a study~~ – studied ~~participated in a meeting~~ – met ~~makes the assumption~~ – assumes
Unnecessary prepositional phrases	
• Change to a possessive	The main point **of the study** **The study's** main point
• Change into an adverb	The reaction occurred **with rapidity**. The reaction **rapidly** occurred.
• Omit when possible	The results **for this case** confirm the hypothesis. The results confirm the hypothesis.

Problem	Correction
Repeated words and phrases	~~Profitable companies, **which generate a lot of money**, have six **different characteristic** traits.~~ Profitable companies have six traits.
Expletive constructions • Avoid phrases such as it + to be, there + to be, and here + to be when used as fillers.	~~**There are** three ways in which statistics are misused.~~ Statistics are misused in three ways.
Nominalizations • These are nouns derived from verbs, adjectives, or adverbs. Express these words in their base forms. ~~decision~~ – decide ~~explanation~~ – explain ~~meeting~~ – meet	~~**The decision** by the committee was to reduce costs.~~ The committee **decided** to reduce costs.
Precision • Use specific quantities, and check words that have similar spelling but different meanings. Terms must express caution.	~~Roughly half of the participants were first year social science students, and the remainders were first year humanities students.~~ All participants were first year students: 14 in social sciences and 16 in humanities. ~~The weather **effected** the participant numbers.~~ The weather **affected** the participant numbers. ~~The results **prove** that~~ – The results **suggest** that

Activity 1

Rewrite the following sentences following effective professional writing techniques.

1. It was ten participants who filled out the online survey.

   _____

   _____

2. The suspects were taken into custody by the police.

   _____

   _____

3. The investigation of the researchers was about the link between caffeine and headaches.

_____

_____

4. The crux of the report is the advertising campaign facilitated an increase in product sales.

_____

_____

5. The results are proof that crimes by juveniles have increased over the past six months.

_____

_____

6. Disappointingly, the intervention group scored lower than the control group.

_____

_____

7. Participants' performance was negatively affected when they experienced high stress and tension because they scored lower on the exam.

_____

_____

8. It is the opinion of the researchers of the study that the participants who have forgone the foremost meal at the outset of the day lacked the energy necessary to increase their cognizant levels which resulted in doing poorly on the exam.

_____

_____

12 Italics and Quotation Marks

Writers communicate with their readers in a variety of ways. While not absolutely necessary, writers may decide to use italics and quotation marks to bring attention to certain parts of a piece of writing. Sometimes these techniques show the noted letters, words, or phrases are being used in a particular or unique way, and sometimes they are key terms for understanding the content. You only need to use italics or quotation marks the first time you write the word, and you should employ these techniques sparingly in your writing, or they will lose their impact for readers.

When to Italicize:

1. Emphasising words
Example: Students must *not* plagiarize.

2. Technical terms
Example: *Proprioception* refers to spatial awareness of one's limbs and body because joints, tendons, and muscles are integrated with the body's central nervous system.

3. Non-English words not accepted as English words
Example: Many Eastern Europeans make *paska*, a sweet bread topped with a light frosting, for Easter.

Signpost See page 196 for using non-English words.

When to Use Quotation Marks:

1. Letters as letters (can also be written in italics)
Example: British English often retains the "re" spelling of French words brought into English.

2. Words as words (can also be written in italics)
Example: In the 1950s, people began using the word "cat" to describe a trendy person.

3. Non-standard or unusual use of a word
Example: The gang leader told his subordinates to make sure their competitor "disappeared."

4. Sarcasm or irony

Example: While searching the Internet for health information, people often encounter dubious medical "experts."

5. Regional or new words which may be unfamiliar to readers:

Example: In Saskatchewan, central Canada, a hooded sweater is often called a "bunny hug."

Activity 1

Identify which part of each sentence writers might want to highlight. If the letter or word should be italicized, underline it. Otherwise, add quotation marks. There may be more than one answer depending on what the writer wants to communicate.

1. Koreans called her a foreigner, but she was born and raised in Korea.

2. On, in, and at are prepositions students still have problems understanding.

3. Cathy was unhappy when people spelled her name with a k.

4. The academy promised rigorous courses, but the students never needed to do homework.

5. In the Mahayana Buddhist tradition, sunyata refers to the intrinsic emptiness of all things.

6. The professor was nice when she assigned four assignments before the holidays.

7. Sujata is very angry because her daughter broke her favourite plate.

8. Many Western monarchies determined power succession through primogeniture, or the custom of a firstborn son inheriting his father's wealth and position.

9. Canadians call their one-dollar coin a loonie because it has a picture of a loon on it.

10. The term genie has Arabic origins.

Logical Fallacies

When presenting an argument, it is vital to be logical and this requires an understanding of common logical mistakes. The following are logical fallacies that can often be found in articles, essays and arguments. Familiarity with them will help you to avoid them in your own work and identify them in information presented to you. Match the definitions with the names in the box.

1._____: **The writer relies on the status of someone who agrees with their opinion as evidence that they are right.** Using the name of a well-respected or successful person to support your argument is only appropriate if they are qualified to speak with authority on the topic. Remember that sometimes authorities are wrong so using a respected name does not prove that you are right.

2._____: **The writer criticizes the person who has the opposite opinion instead of the reasons for their opinion.** Remember that even bad people can be right, and not liking someone is not a reason to think they are wrong.

3._____: **The writer compares the main idea to something else, but the comparison is weak or inappropriate.** Analogies are very useful to help make a point clear, but they must match the relevant details of the topic.

4._____: **The writer assumes that only two opinions are possible, usually a good one and a bad one.** They do not consider ideas in the middle of the two extremes or any other possible opinions.

5._____: **The writer uses their conclusion or opinion to support the premise.** In other words, the premise is the same as the conclusion.

6._____: **The writer confuses correlation for cause and effect.** They connect two events by saying that the second must have been caused by the first. Of course, while outcomes are caused by preceding events, the time sequence doesn't prove causation.

7._____: **The writer assumes that one event or action will lead to far more serious events.** The aim is usually to scare the reader. Remember that the more serious actions on the slope are things that most people can still choose to avoid and are not really inevitable outcomes of choosing the milder action.

8._____: **The writer explains the opposite viewpoint but adds or removes details to make it seem weaker or ridiculous.** The aim is to pretend to have considered the other side, but really to have misrepresented it. Remember to research opposing opinions by reading what the opponents really say, and when you use a counterargument in your writing, give appropriate context so you present the ideas accurately.

9._____: **The writer says that if you can't disprove something then it must be true.** This might be that the writer has not seen evidence against their own position, or it could be that their opponents have not definitively shown that the idea is true or false. This is a form of shifting the burden of proof, or saying that the writer's opinion is right and the evidence is the lack of evidence against it.

10._____: **The writer says that an idea is right because it is popular.** Of course, lots of popular ideas are wrong and it can be hard to gauge popularity. A hundred people might seem to make an idea popular, but not if there are a million who oppose them.

Argument from authority	Faulty analogy
Argument from ignorance	Bandwagon
False dichotomy	Begging the question
Ad hominem	Slippery slope
Post hoc ergo propter hoc	Straw man

Activity 1

Read the following paragraph and identify the logical fallacies.

Games of Death

Violent video games should be banned because they cause people to be violent. Society has become so obsessed with video games that people are either obsessive gamers or they want video games to be banned. Gamers say that video games do not cause violence, which means they think that games are good for people and everyone should play video games. Psychologist Christine Ferguson says that her research shows no clear link between video games and violence, although she cannot know about violence because she has a good job and lives in a safe neighborhood. Furthermore, her research did not include all violent games, and she did not study the effects on all children, so it does not prove that violent games never make anyone violent. She says that her children are allowed to play violent games, but would she let her children play with real guns or take drugs? If people let their children play violent video games, then they will let them play with real guns, and eventually children will be allowed to kill people in real life. John Ryan, a retired police officer, saw lots of violence in his career, so his opinion is stronger than that of a psychologist. Ryan is convinced that video games cause violence, and he says, "My three grandsons play shooting games, and they fight with each other all the time, so the connection is clear." He goes on to say, "If they play video games at night, they will probably fight with each other the next day." An online poll of concerned parents recently showed that 60% of people agree that violence is linked to video games, and this strongly supports my call for violent games to be banned. In conclusion, since people like me think that violent games should be banned, violent games must be dangerous to society; therefore such video games should be banned.

1) Underline the logical fallacies in the paragraph and identify each one with the appropriate number from the list on page 213.

_____

_____

2) What other logical fallacies do you know? Discuss them with your partner and give some examples.

_____

_____

Activity 2

In your notebook, write a paragraph of your own including some logical fallacies. Exchange your writing with your partner and try to identify the logical fallacies they have used.

14 Paraphrasing and Summarizing

In academic writing, writers often integrate information from other sources in order to support their own ideas and opinions. Paraphrasing and summarizing are ways of incorporating ideas from other sources without using the exact words.

What Is Paraphrasing?

Paraphrasing is rewording and rearranging the content of text without changing the meaning or dramatically altering the length. It is useful alternative to a direct quotation when using information from another source, and it is a valuable skill that is used in the writing process.

Example:
Original text (21 words)

In his prime, soccer star Wayne Rooney was a machine designed for sport. His stocky, powerful physique made him more powerful than his opponents.

Paraphrased version (23 words)

At his peak, Wayne Rooney—a famous soccer player—had a powerful body, which made him a stronger soccer player than the players he competed against.

Summarized version (10 words)
Wayne Rooney's powerful body made him a soccer legend.

How to Paraphrase

There are three main steps in the processes of paraphrasing:

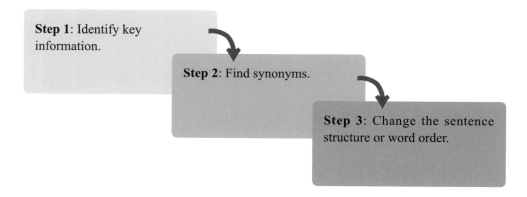

Step 1: Identify key information.

Step 2: Find synonyms.

Step 3: Change the sentence structure or word order.

Example 2:

Original text

An article in *GQ* magazine reports that actor David DeMotto is considering retirement from the movie business due to an undisclosed medical condition.

Step 1: Identify key information.

Read the text carefully and highlight or underline the important words to change.

An article in *GQ* magazine **reports** that **actor** David DeMotto is **considering** retirement from the **movie business** due to an **undisclosed medical condition**.

Step 2: Find synonyms.

Report	rumour, state, disclose, reveal
Actor	film star, thespian, performer, player
Considering	thinking about, contemplating, planning on
Movie business	film industry, acting
Undisclosed	unnamed, unidentified, secret
Medical condition	health problem, personal reason

New sentence:

An article in *GQ* magazine reveals that film star David DeMotto is thinking about retirement from the film industry due to health problems.

Step 3: Change the sentence structure.

Paraphrase 1:

Film star David DeMotto is thinking about retirement from the film industry due to health problems, according to an article in *GQ* magazine.

Paraphrase 2:

Due to health problems, film star David DeMotto is thinking about retirement from the film industry, according to an article in *GQ* magazine.

Signpost See page 12-20 for more information on sentence types.

Activity 1

Rewrite the following sentences by following steps 1–3.

1. The little boy named Sam was very nervous about his test; as a result, he vomited.

   _____

   _____

2. The rural school could not afford to buy new computers, for they were not cheap.

   _____

   _____

3. Although Nak Kyun stayed up all night writing his essay, he had too many grammar mistakes to get a good mark.

   _____

   _____

4. Children between the ages of 9 and 12 study for an average of five hours every week outside of normal school hours.

   _____

   _____

5. It is against the law for teachers to use corporal punishment in schools in New Zealand.

   _____

   _____

6. Learning English is very important for entrance into good schools and more opportunities in the workplace.

   _____

   _____

7. *FourFourTwo* Magazine described Park Ji-sung as one of the best Asian players to have played in the English Premier League.

   _____

   _____

8. South Korean group BTS became the first K-pop group to top the U.S. Billboard 200 charts.

   _____

   _____

What Is Summarizing?

Like paraphrasing, summarizing involves rewording and rearranging the content of a text without changing the meaning, but the writer dramatically reduces the length to provide an overview of the original text. This is particularly useful when a writer wishes to focus on the main idea without including examples, statistics, and details.

How to summarize

There are three main steps in the processes of summarizing:

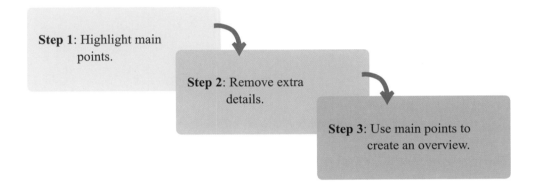

Example:
Original text (118 words)

In his prime, soccer star Wayne Rooney was a machine designed for sports. His stocky, powerful physique made him more powerful than his opponents. At a height of 176cm, Rooney had a low center of gravity, which enabled him to change direction quickly at pace, and outmaneuver bigger defenders. His upper body strength was a considerable asset, and allowed him to hold-off other players while controlling the ball. Although not gifted with electric pace, Rooney's leg strength allowed him to kick the ball with remarkable force, which is a great asset as a striker. Because of these physical attributes and never-say-die attitude, Rooney is considered one of the best players to have played the game.

Step 1: Highlight the main points

In his prime, soccer star **Wayne Rooney** was a machine designed for sports. His stocky, powerful physique made him **more powerful than his opponents**. At a height of 176cm, Rooney had a **low center of gravity**, which enabled him to change direction quickly at pace, and outmaneuver bigger defenders. His **upper body strength** was a considerable asset, and allowed him to hold off other players while controlling the ball. Although not gifted with electric pace, Rooney's **leg strength** allowed him to kick the ball with remarkable force, which is a great asset as a striker. Because of these physical attributes and never-say-die attitude, Rooney is considered **one of the best players** to have played the game.

Step 2: Remove extra details

Wayne Rooney
more powerful than his opponents
low centre of gravity
upper body strength
leg strength
one of the best players

Step 3: Summarized version (9 words)

Wayne Rooney's powerful body made him a soccer legend.

Activity 2

Now try to summarize the following information into one sentence using steps 1–3.

> The rate of birth in South Korea fell to the second lowest in the world. Only Hong Kong has a lower birthrate. There are many reasons why so many couples hesitate to have children. One problem is that there are not enough childcare facilities in Korea. The other issue is that education costs for children are on the rise.

_____

_____

_____

> Although Korean adults have one of the lowest levels of obesity in the world, Korean children are getting heavier. A recent study from the Institute for Childhood Nutrition shows 1 in 10 children are obese, and a larger number are overweight. Because of the university entrance exam, even young students spend an increasing amount of time sitting in their chairs studying at home, at afterschool programs, and at their regular public schools. In addition, instead of a diet full of fresh vegetables and fruit, children today eat more junk or instant food than ever before. _Ramyeon_, chips, frozen pre-prepared meals, and hamburgers or French fries have now replaced well balanced, homemade meals for children.

_____

_____

_____

_____

Activity 3

Use the three summarizing steps to change each paragraph into one sentence.

Homeschooling

There are several different reasons why students are homeschooled. Some religious families feel that their children need an education that is more focused on their beliefs. Other parents are worried about negative influences in public schools such as smoking, drugs, bullying, or other forms of violence. There are also children who do not fit in with the regular school system because they are either gifted children who learn faster than regular students or because they have learning disabilities or learn slower than other students. Thus, there is no one reason why parents decide to homeschooled their children.

_____

_____

Because homeschooling is so different from public schools, some people have concerns about children learning at home. Unlike mainstream schools where children are exposed to a diversity of people and opinions from different teachers and interacting with other students, homeschooled children have only their parents' perspectives or the curriculum's perspective, which was probably chosen by the parents. In addition, children might not be well socialized with mainstream society. As a result, homeschooled children might not be able to fit well into the rest of the community later in life.

_____

_____

Despite these problems, there are also benefits to homeschooling. First, children who are very talented or are experiencing learning disabilities can learn at their own pace at home. Children who excel at languages, science, or other subjects can devote more time to their area or areas of interest, and those students may one day be great linguists or scientists because of their extra studies; on the other hand, students who are struggling in one area can devote more time to reading skills, mathematics, or whatever subject they need to improve. The second advantage is that children can have a closer relationship with their parents because they spend much more time with their parents than in the traditional education system. Likewise, parents who teach their children are much more involved in their education, and they can help guide their children in life and education.

_____

_____

💡 Grammar Tip

If paraphrasing or summarizing from another source, you must include an in-text citation in order to indicate clearly where you found the original information. See pages 225-228 for more information on in-text citations.

Research Skills

Students often hear that they should not plagiarize or copy someone else's work, but they do not always have the skills to avoid replicating previously published work. This section gives students practical skills to both avoid plagiarism and make their writing assignments stronger by incorporating outside evidence into their work. Students will first learn what plagiarim is and how they can correctly incorporate in-text citations and quotations. Finally, they will learn how to cite sources used in their writing.

This section covers:

- Research and Writing
- In-Text Citations
- Quotations
- Works Cited

1 Research and Writing

In academic writing, it is not enough just to provide your own ideas and opinions. Good academic writing involves the development of the writer's ideas with support from other credible authors and sources.

When writers provide information from other sources, they must provide the reader with proper documentation of all the information used. If writers take information without acknowledging it, they are guilty of plagiarism.

What Is Plagiarism?

Plagiarism is taking information and ideas from other sources and claiming them to be yours. By not acknowledging the source(s), the writer is committing literary theft.

In example 1, Student A has taken information from the author H.J. Chang but has not acknowledged it. The writer is claiming that the idea is his/her own. This is plagiarism.

> **Example 1**: Culture influences a country's economic performance. A particular culture may produce people with certain behavioral traits.

In example 2, the student has correctly acknowledged the original author and avoided plagiarism.

> **Example 2**: According to H.J. Chang, Professor of Economics at Cambridge University, "Culture influences a country's economic performance. At a given point in time, a particular culture may produce people with particular behavioral traits that are more conducive to achieving certain goals, including economic development, than other countries" (200).

Writers are also guilty of plagiarism if they attempt to paraphrase too closely (put into your own words) information from another source. In example 3, while the writer does not use the exact words from the author, the paraphrase is too closely related to the original. Again, the source is not cited.

> **Example 3: Culture** can affect **a country's economic performance**. Over time, **a particular culture may produce people with** certain **behavior traits**.

How Can Writers Avoid Plagiarism?

When using information from other sources, the source(s) must always be acknowledged. By providing an accurate and full description of the sources used, the writer can avoid plagiarism. This is done in two ways:

1. By providing a parenthetical citation, called an **in-text citation**, within the text. This is where the author's name and page number is provided in parenthesis at the end of the borrowed information (MLA Style).

> **Example 1**: The Maori language spoken by the indigenous people of New Zealand is closely related to Hawaiian Tahitian (Tane 196).

In this example, the reader can see the information came from page 196 and is written by the author Tane.

2. By providing a **Works Cited** page at the end of the writing that provides the reader a more comprehensive record of the source.

> **Example 2**: Tane, John. *The History of the Maori Language*. Wellington: Whitcombe and Tombs, 2006.

In the Works Cited page, the reader can find out the full name of the author, the title of the source, and the publishing details.

Is There a Format or Style That I Should Follow When Making In-text Citations and a Works Cited Page?

Depending on whom you are writing for and the type of writing you are doing, different documentation styles can be used. Below are just a few of the many styles used in writing:
- APA Style (American Psychological Association)
- Chicago Style
- Harvard Style
- MLA Style (Modern Language Association)

This book will follow the MLA Style; however, it is important to check with your professor or department to find out which style they prefer or use.

2 In-Text Citations

How Do I Create an In-text Citation?

In an in-text citation, the works of others are acknowledged using a parenthetical citation. This involves placing the name(s) of the author(s), page number(s), or both in parentheses ( ). When an author is unknown, a partial title is included inside of the parentheses. In all cases, a parenthetical citation should be written at the end of any sentence where the work of another is used.

An in-text citation gives the reader a trail to follow should they wish to find out more information on the source(s) used in the text.

1. **Basic entry**: Place the author(s)'s family name(s) and/or page number(s) in parenthesis at the end of the sentence.

> **Example 1**: When developing countries are faced with a payment crisis, "Signing an agreement with the IMF is crucial" (Chang 145).
>
> **Example 2**: According to Chang, "Signing an agreement with the IMF is crucial," when developing countries are faced with a payment crisis (145).

If the reader wants more information on the source, he or she can go to the works cited page and find the full reference:

Chang, Ha Joon. *Bad Samaritans: The Myth of Free Trade and the Secret History of Capitalism.* Bloomsbury Press, 2008.

2. **A source with multiple authors**: If a source has multiple authors, state the names. If the source has two authors, list the authors' last names as they appear with the page number. With more than three authors, use the first author's family name followed by et al. (Latin for "and others").

> **Example 3**: The Arabica coffee bean is commonly used for breakfast blends because of its moderate aroma and body (Kim et al. 31).

3. **Authors with the same family name**: If the authors have the same family name, use the first initials of both authors.

Example 4: Researchers address this in various ways, stating, "Tougher laws are necessary to battle the growing social problems associated with drugs in South Korea" (J.H. Kim), and, "Increased vigilance at South Korea's import hubs will have some impact on the [drug] problem" (T.K. Kim).

Example 5: S.H. Park argues that tougher drug laws are vital in fighting the battle against crime (17). This view is also supported by Seoul metropolitan police who reported that drug related crimes have increased by 7% from the last year (J.S. Park 27).

4. **No page number**: If using an internet or digital source that does not include a page number, simply include the author's family name in the parentheses.

5. **No author**: If the author is not known, use the title of the work instead of the author. Titles of webpages and articles should be written inside quotation marks " ".

Example 6: After the recent data hacking attacks at SK Telecom, many people are nervous about placing personal information online ("Time to Hit the Reset Button").

6. **Corporate or government authors**: If the work is created by a company or government agency, include the name of the country or company followed by the department name and page number(s).

Example 7: The eastern coast of South Korea "has a relatively straight, featureless coastline" which a tidal height difference of only 30 cm (Republic of Korea, Ministry of Culture, Sports and Tourism).

7. **Emphasis on the author**: If the author of the work is emphasized in a sentence, then only put the page number or partial title of the source in parentheses.

Example 8: Motivational speaker Jim Rohn argues that "Success is the continual unfolding of the design of your own life and pulling it off" ("Guide to Time Management").

8. **Indirect source**: If a quote or idea by one author is mentioned in a work by another author, add the words qtd. in before the author's name or article title.

> **Example 9**: Steve Jobs, co-founder and former CEO of Apple, was not a fan of the stylus. He once famously declared, "God gave us 10 styluses. Let's not invent another one" (qtd. in Goldman).

9. **Constitution and laws**: When citing from a country's constitution or rules of law, introduce any information by clearly emphasizing the source in the sentence and indicating articles, chapters, sections, clauses, or amendments in parentheses.

> **Example 10**: The Korean Constitution clearly states that "The sovereignty of the Republic of Korea shall reside in the people, and all state authority shall emanate from the people" (Ch. 1, Art. 1, Sec. 2).

Source	Citation
One author	(Kim 123)
Multiple authors	(Kim and Park 123) (Kim et al. 123)
Authors with the same family name	(J.H. Kim, T.K. Kim 3)
Internet source	If author and page number (Kim 123) No author or page number ("partial article name")
No author	(*Book title* 123) ("Article title" 123)
Corporate or government agency	(Hyundai Motors 36) (Republic of Korea, Ministry of Economy and Finance)
Indirect source	(qtd. in Lee 367)

Activity 3

In-text citations are most easily determined based on the complete works cited citations that appear at the end of an essay. Use the works cited citations below to create in-text citations.

1. Kim Ja-in, an internationally renowned Korean climbing champion, is scheduled to scale the 555-meter tall Lotte World Tower this Saturday (   ).

   Ko, Dong-hwan. "'Human Spider' to Climb Lotte World Tower with Bare Hands on May 20 [VIDEO]." *The Korea Times*, 16 May 20XX, www.koreatimes.co.kr/www/ sports/20XX/05/663_229437.html.

2. An Asiana Airlines aircraft collided with a Turkish jet on the runway at Ataturk International Airport in Istanbul, Turkey on Sunday. The accident caused a brief fire on the Turkish plane but no one was injured (   ).

   "No Injuries as Asiana Jet Collides with Turkish Plane on Istanbul Runway." The Chosun Ilbo, 15 May 20XX, english.chosun.com/site/data/html_dir/20XX/ 05/15/2018051500629.html.

3. On one cold day in 1914, Thomas Edison's research laboratory caught fire and entire buildings were engulfed in flames. Yet Edison was unfazed. He calmly told his son to find his mother and tell her and her friends to come quickly. "They'll never see a fire like this again" (   ). (Hint: on page 150)

   Holiday, Ryan. "Love Everything That Happens: Amor Fati." The Obstacle Is the Way. Portfolio, 20XX, p. 150-155.

What Is a Quotation?

A quotation is essentially the acknowledgement of words and ideas from another author or source. Every time you use information from another source, you need to clearly show your reader where it comes from. Sometimes writers use indirect quotations (paraphrased or summarized ideas), and sometimes they choose to use direct quotations (the exact words taken from another person or source).

When Should I Use a Quotation?

Both direct and indirect quotations can be valuable tools in strengthening your own writing but should never be over-used. The aim is to use quotations to expand or support your own ideas. If you find yourself citing most sentences in your assignment, you are not using enough of your own ideas and analysis.

Some writers also have difficulty determining when to source information. Generally, if the information is common knowledge that the writer knows without having to do research, the information does not need an in-text citation. However, if the writer needs to do research to find out either the words or ideas, the information needs an in-text citation.

Activity 1

Look at the following sentences. Mark the sentences with an X if the information comes from the author's general knowledge. This information does not need an in-text citation.

1. Unemployment is an important issue these days. Source: Newspaper article

2. The unemployment rate rose by 1.5% which is the fastest increase in the past two years. Source: Government statistics

3. In the name of Allah, the Entirely Merciful, the Especially Merciful. Source: Qur'an., Al-Fatiha 1.1

4. Fair is foul, and foul is fair. Source: Macbeth 1.1.13

5. Everyone has the right to be secure against unreasonable search or seizure. Source: Canadian Charter of Rights and Freedoms Section 8

6. 42% of students polled said they wanted the quality of food to improve in the cafeteria. Source: University survey

7. Korean society puts a lot of emphasis on education. Source: Magazine article

8. Democracy grinds to a halt without a willingness to compromise, or when even basic

facts are contested, or when we listen only to those who agree with us. Our public life withers when only the most extreme voices get all the attention. Source: President Obama's State of the Union Address – Government Archives

9. "Canada" comes from an Iroquois word meaning "the village." Source: Internet encyclopaedia

10. Sungkyunkwan University is a Confucian university. Source: University website

Indirect vs. Direct Quotations

An indirect quotation retains the ideas from the original author while changing the words and sentence structure or order. As the writer does not use the exact words from the source, quotation marks are not used.

A direct quotation is where the writer takes the exact words from an author and places them in quotation marks (" ").

In both cases, the author or source needs to be acknowledged, and the sources require an in-text citation and entry in the Works Cited page at the end of the assignment. Reporting verbs are used in both types of quotations.

Original Source: A healthy diet is vital for optimum performance in sport. (Source: David Johnson, page 34)

Indirect Quotation: David Johnson, a leading expert in sports nutrition, argues that to perform at the highest level in sports, a nutritious diet is important (34).

Direct Quotation: David Johnson, a leading expert in sports nutrition, argues, "A healthy diet is vital for optimum performance in sport" (34).

Reporting Verbs with Direct and Indirect Quotations

There are a number of verbs which are helpful for introducing quotations. These are called reporting verbs. The following are some common reporting verbs and phrases:

* According to	Claim	Emphasize	Maintain	Report
Agree	Declare	Highlight	Mention	Say
Argue	Define	Identify	Predict	State
Ask	Describe	Insist	Propose	Suggest
Assert	Demonstrate	Indicate	Recommend	

* Most reporting verbs follow the subject such as "Smith argues", but *According* to precedes the subject such as "According to Smith."

Writers also need to decide if they should use an indirect or direct quotation when incorporating other sources. In general, direct quotations are only used when the words themselves are important. For example, writers might want to quote the words of a relevant law, a dictionary definition, or a primary source such as a piece of literature or religious text. However, indirect quotations are used when the idea or information is more important than the words. For instance, data is usually put into an indirect quotation instead of a direct quotation. Statements from experts can be made into either indirect or direct quotations depending on the information and circumstances.

Activity 2

Look again at the sentences on pages 229-230. If information does need to be referenced in an in-text citation, decide if it would be better as an indirect quote (I) or direct quote (D).

How to Write an Indirect Quotation

Signpost See pages 216-221 for paraphrasing and summarizing.

How to Write a Direct Quotation

1. Introduce the source

Explain where the quote comes from to show why the source is authoritative. For example, this information could include the name and background of the author, the organization which conducted the research, or the name of the source.

Example 1: Jane Yu, a leading language expert at South University, argues, "The most effective way of testing a learner's pronunciation is to observe and record the learner performing in a variety of situations" (95).

2. Incorporate the quote

Integrate the author's words into your own sentence, and place a period after the in-text citation (basic information about where the source comes from). If the quotation includes a question mark or exclamation mark, place it before the end mark. Reporting verbs require a comma, but commas are not necessary when introducing a quotation with other words.

Example 2: Education expert Fernando Lewis claims that "Play is the mode through which children encounter and explore knowledge" (201).

Example 3: The first question in a survey conducted by the Center for Better Education asked, "How satisfied are you with the quality of teaching at your university?" (3).

3. Capitalize correctly

Capitalize the first word in a quotation. With a broken quotation, capitalize the first word in the first set of quotation marks, but do not capitalize the first word in the second set of quotation marks.

Example 4: First Choice's employee policy handbook states, "Employees may be terminated if they post material on personal social media accounts which is deemed inappropriate or harmful to the company" (31).

Example 5: "Memorization has a place in language learning," says Professor Bora Lee, "but students need opportunities to practice and use their skills to develop true competency" (42).

Sometimes additional steps are necessary to use direct quotes correctly.

1. Remove unnecessary information

Unnecessary information may need to be removed from a quote to reduce wordiness. When omitting a word, phrase, or sentence from a longer passage, use an ellipsis (three spaced periods) to tell the reader that the quoted material is part of a longer text.

Example 6: (Original) Public health official Dr. Sabrina Mamuji said, "Diet related issues are now one of the leading causes of preventable death. People need to exercise daily such as walking, running, cycling, weight lifting, playing team sports, or doing other forms of cardiovascular exercise to reduce their risk of early death" (5).

Example 7: (Reduced quote) Public health official Dr. Sabrina Mamuji said, "Diet related issues are now one of the leading causes of preventable death. People need to exercise daily . . . to reduce their risk of early death" (5).

2. Remove unnecessary information after a full sentence

When a fully quoted sentence is followed by a partial sentence, it may appear as if there is a four dot ellipsis. However, because the full sentence needs to end with a period, the missing portion of the quote in the following sentence is noted through an ellipsis. The two sentences are merged into one. Thus, there are four dots in a row.

Example 8: (Original) "Children require hours of daily play. They have evolved in this way without which they are unable to develop properly," explained psychologist Ivan Applegate.

Example 9: (Reduced quote) "Children require hours of daily play. . . . without which they are unable to develop properly," explained psychologist Ivan Applegate.

3. Mark errors in a quote

On occasion, there is a grammar, spelling, or vocabulary mistake in the original quote. Since direct quotes cannot be changed, writers use [sic] to show the mistake. However, [sic] is not used for different varieties of English such as spelling differences in American and British English.

Example: The Ministry of Education sent out a tweet stating, "Its [sic] imperative that our students demonstrate grammar competency."

4. Edit a quotation for clarity

When a quote is removed from its original context, sometimes important information such as the subject or location may become unclear. In this case, writers need to insert clarifying information in square brackets.

Unclear example: "He should resign immediately," said the United Party leader.

Clearer example: "[Alexander de Pfeffel] should resign immediately," said the United Party leader.

Activity 3

Correct the following direct quotes.

1. David Digby, the head of space exploration at NASA, mentioned "Soon we will be able to send a kangaroo to the moon." (29)

2. "Eating red meet every day results in many health risks," says nutritionist Lindsay Truong.

3. The University of Kingston dormitory policy states that, "students who do not pay residence fees in full by the deadline will not be guaranteed a room on campus" (4).

4. "People must learn to live within their means," argues financial expert Enes Claw, "If they wish to reduce personal debt" (88).

5. Climate scientist Dr. Rusty Pitt raised an interesting question when he asked, "Are we not all to blame for the increase in global warming"? (45).

6. Jisu Kim, my mother, said, "The world is set for another recession."

7. "As the oldest university in Korea, it has an important role to play in educating the public about the history of education in the nation," said Confucian Heritage head Oh Hee Choi.

Activity 4

Look at the following direct quote, and decide where an ellipsis could be used to eliminate unnecessary information.

1. Global Books issued a statement that said, "Due to several factors including rising wages, declining in-store sales, increasing on-line sales, and changing demographics, we have decided to close our store location and move our business entirely online" (1).

_____

_____

_____

_____

_____

_____

Analyzing Direct Quotations

Once a direct quotation has been properly contextualized, sourced, and incorporated into the writer's sentence, there is one more step that needs to be completed. Because direct quotations are used to support the author's point, they cannot merely appear in an assignment. They also need to be analyzed or discussed to show why the quotation is important in the context of the assignment.

Example:

The main theme of Shakespeare's *Macbeth* is established in the first scene. As the play opens, the scheming Weird Sisters chant, "Fair is foul, and foul is fair" (1.1.13). On one level, this means that appearances can deceive both characters and the audience. However, it also means that what is good can turn bad and vice versa.

Activity 5

Looking at the example above, complete the following steps:

1. Underline the background of the quote.

2. Circle all of the punctuation that incorporates the quote into the writer's own sentence.

3. Highlight the in-text citation with another colour.

4. Draw a box around the analysis.

Activity 6

Incorporate these sentences into your own, and analyze the meaning of the text using the model example above.

"All citizens shall be assured of their human worth and dignity and shall have the right to pursue happiness. It shall be the duty of the State to confirm and guarantee the fundamental and inviolable human rights of individuals." – Constitution of the Republic of Korea, Chapter 2, Article 10

_____

_____

_____

_____

Activity 7

In your notebook, write a paragraph that develops the topic given below. Use quotations for support. You do not need to use all the information provided.

Topic: University and the influence of peers

Topic Sentence: The relationship with peers is critical during university life.

Book 1

Author: Dr. Min Jee Park (psychologist)

Title: *Necessary Networks: The Case for University Peer Groups*

1 – 63% of university students say their peers are more influential in helping them make life decisions than parents (23).

2 – University students who have supportive friendship networks are 42% less likely to have mental health problems (45).

3 - There is no greater predictor for mental well-being during university than a solid peer network (88).

Author: Cynthia Lee (economist)

Title: *The Ties that Bind: University Networks and the World of Work*

1 - 55% of university seniors found their first job through peer networks (12).

2 – The relationships students forge during their university years have a significant impact on their future career (91).

3 - Six in 10 adults in their 40s are still in close contact with their university friends (117).

4 Works Cited

How Do I Create a Works Cited Page?

The Works Cited page is the last part of your paper and contains a reference of every source used in the paper.

Look at the following example of a Works Cited page.

Works Cited

Chang, Ha Joon. *Bad Samaritans: The Myth of Free Trade and the Secret History of Capitalism*. Bloomsbury Press, 2009.

Cheon, Du-shin, et al. "2020 대학평가" ["2020 University Rankings"]. *JoongAng Ilbo*, 6 Oct. 2020, news.joins.com/article/127843456.

Davies, John, et al. *Capitalism in Africa*. Atlas House, 2020.

Gilbert, Nellie, and Jacqueline Rousseau. "Money and Power" *Time*. 30 May 2019, pp. 67-71.

Goldman, David. "Steve Jobs on Stylus: 'Over My Dead Body.' The Pencil and Four Other Things He Would Hate." *CNN Money*, 10 Sept. 2015, money.cnn.com/2015/09/10/technology/apple-pencil-steve-jops-stylus.index.html.

Kinesthesia4u. "The Power of Numbers." *YouTube*, 25 Jan. 2021, youtu.be/fkghsygekgu54c.

Republic of Korea. Ministry of Finance and Economy. Dept. of Fiscal Policy. *Balancing the Books in the New Millennium*. Seoul: 2001.

"20 Things Wrong with Facebook." *Social Media Critic*, 5 Dec. 2020, socialmediacritic2020.com/facebook/20-things.html.

Wilburg, Jessie. *Asia's Economic Miracle*. Discover 21, 2016.

---. *The History of Capitalism in Asia*. Discover 21, 2015.

Activity 1

1. How many different sources are used?

2. Which source(s) can be found online?

3. Which source(s) has/have more than two authors?

4. Which source(s) were created by unknown authors?

Is There a Certain Format I Should Follow?

Like the rest of your writing, the Works Cited page follows a format. The format is as follows:

1. The Works Cited page begins on a new page and is numbered, continuing from the last page in the essay.
2. There is a centered title which is 2.5 cm from the top of the page. The title is separated from the first entry (source) by two lines.
3. Like the rest of the paper, the Works Cited page has margins.
4. The Works Cited page has a hanging indentation. This means that if an entry is more than one line, the subsequent line(s) is/are indented from the left margin by 1.3 cm.
5. Double space all entries.
6. Entries follow alphabetical order.
7. Numbers at the beginning of titles should be treated as they are spelled (e.g., "20 Things" is alphabetized as "Twenty Things").
8. If two or more works by an author are cited, write their name on the first line as normal, but also add three dashes – – – to the beginning of each new entry by the same author.

Arranging Entries in the Works Cited Page

MLA requires up to nine core elements to be included in a Works Cited citation. In most cases, only a few of the nine elements are used. The nine elements in order are:

1. Author.
2. Title of source.
3. Title of container,
4. Other contributors,
5. Version,
6. Number,
7. Publisher,
8. Publication date,
9. Location.

1. **Author**: This can be either a person's true name or an online nickname (common on blogs and YouTube).
2. **Title of source**: This is usually the title of a book, article, webpage, or movie. It can be either italicized (for major works such as movies, books, and albums) or in quotation marks (for articles, chapters, songs, and episodes).

3. **Title of container**: A container is like a supertitle. For example, a TV show name would be the container for an episode name; similarly, a book title is a container for a book chapter.

4. **Other contributors**: This can include the names of editors, illustrators, translators, and other helpers.

5. **Version**: This information is necessary when there are multiple versions of a book, such as the Bible.

6. **Number**: This is either the edition of the book or the specific volume of a collection of books.

7. **Publisher**: If the title of the source is the same as the publisher, then the publisher may be omitted (e.g., *CNN*, ~~CNN~~).

8. **Publication date**: For books, this is the year that a book is first published, not printed. The most recent date that an article or webpage has been updated should be used as the publication date. In some cases, no date is visible so this element may be omitted.

9. **Location**: This can be either a group of page numbers (used for sections of a book) or a URL.

1. Book by a single author

> Author's family name, given name. *Title of the book*. Publisher name, year of publication.

Publisher name: You can exclude the word "Books" or "Press" (e.g., Penguin vs Penguin Books) but make sure to include UP if the publisher is a university press (e.g., Sungkyunkwan UP).

> **Example 1**: Chang, Ha Joon. *Bad Samaritans: The Myth of Free Trade and the Secret History of Capitalism*. Bloomsbury, 2009.

2. A book with more than one author

Give the authors details following from how they appear on the title page. For the first auhor, place the family name first as per a single entry, but for a second author, put the given name first followed by the family name. If there are three or more authors, just include et al. after the first author's name is given.

> **Example 2a**: Bracken, Daniel, and Irene Parker. *UFO Abduction*s. Braeburn House, 1996.
> **Example 2b**: Davis, Rian, et al. *Capitalism in Africa*. Atlas House, 2020.

3. An article from a reference book (or online website)

When citing from an encyclopedia or other reference book, give the author (if present), title of the search term in quotation marks, and title of the source.

If no author is provided, then give the title of the section in the reference book, and place it in quotation marks. Follow with the title of the reference book, edition, and year.

Example 3a: "Shanghai." *Encyclopedia Britannica*, 15th ed., 2002.

Example 3b: Boxer, Baruch. "Shanghai." *Encyclopædia Britannica*, www.britannica.com/place/Shanghai

If citing a specific definition from a dictionary, add the abbreviation Def. (definition) and the appropriate number or letter as found in the dictionary. You can direct readers to the specific definition you are citing in an in-text citation (e.g., "Content," def. 3a).

Example 3c: "Content." *Merriam-Webster's Collegiate Dictionary*, 11th ed., Merriam-Webster, 2003, p. 269.

Example 3d: "Content." *Merriam-Webster Dictionary*, merriam-webster.com/dictionary/content.

4. A book with no author

If a book has no author, give the title and then publishing details.

Example 4: *New American Standard Bible*. Foundation Publications, 1995.

5. Government publications

Government publications may have many different sources and therefore need to be treated carefully. If no author is given, cite the government that issued it first, and then the agency or department that published it. Finally, follow normal publishing details.

Example 5: Republic of Korea. Ministry of Commerce, Industry, and Energy. Dept. of Energy. *Energy in the New Millennium*. 2011.

6. A translated book

If a book has been translated, it is necessary to include both an author's name as well as the translator's name, which is included as a contributor.

Example 6: Coehlo, Paulo. *The Alchemist*. Translated by Alan R. Clarke, HarperCollins, 1993.

7. An article in a journal (printed and online)

> Author's name. "Article Title." *Title of Container/Publisher*, Number, Date, Location.

An article in a journal has a different format from a book. The title of the article is placed in quotation marks while the journal title is in italics. The volume number, issue number, year of publication, and inclusive page numbers, all follow the title.

In the case of journals retrieved online, additional information is required: the name of the database (in italics), the URL or DOI (Digital Object Identifier), and finally the date it was accessed.

> **Example 7a**: Hagen, Patricia L., and Thomas W. Zelman. "'We Were Never on the Scene of the Crime': Eavan Boland's Repossession of History." *Twentieth Century Literature*, vol. 37, no. 4, 1991, pp. 442-453.
>
> **Example 7b**: Hagen, Patricia L., and Thomas W. Zelman. "'We Were Never on the Scene of the Crime': Eavan Boland's Repossession of History." *Twentieth Century Literature*, vol. 37, no. 4, 1991, pp. 442-453, *InfoTrac Student Edition*, doi:10.5465/amle/2013/0337. Accessed 19 Nov. 2020.
>
> *Note that 7b has additional information (after the page location) that indicates the journal article was retrieved from an online database.

8. An article in a newspaper (printed and online)

> Author's last name, first name. "Article Title." *Publication details*. Medium of Publication.

If the newspaper is locally published, write the city in square brackets, not underlined, after the newspaper name. Nationally or internationally published newspapers do not need to have the city included. Put the publication in italics and not the title. If the newspaper is in sections (A, B, C) then include the section and pagination. An access date is not required for newspaper articles.

> **Example 8a**: Fitzgerald, Eddie. "A True Sky-High San Francisco Real Estate Crisis." *The Chronicle* [Chicago], 19 Dec. 2019, p. 9.
>
> **Example 8b**: Fitzgerald, Eddie. "A True Sky-High San Francisco Real Estate Crisis." *The Chronicle* [Chicago], 19 Dec. 2019, chichronicle.com/realestate/12-19-2019/sky-high.htm.

9. An article in a magazine (printed and online)

Like a newspaper, italicize the publication, not the article title. Include the complete date after the title of the magazine followed a colon (:) and pagination.

> **Example 9a**: Gibbs, Nancy. "Sex and Power: Why Powerful Men Abuse Women." *Time*, May 2011, pp. 67-71.
>
> **Example 9b**: Gibbs, Nancy. "Sex and Power: Why Powerful Men Abuse Women." *Time*, May 2011, content.time.com/time/magazine/article/0,9171,2072641,00.html.

10. A YouTube Video

Web videos, including those from YouTube, can be cited as a short work from a web site. Start by typing the screenname (user ID), followed by the poster's real name in parentheses, if it is available. Use the exact capitalization and spelling of the screen name (user ID) and title that is found in the original video description.

> **Example 10**: DroneRiot. "Choosing a radio for your drone." *YouTube*, 15 May 2021, www.youtube.com/watch?v=53657367r-t845.

11. A Social Media Post

Begin by stating the writer's screenname (user ID), followed by their real name in parentheses, if it is available. If the post is untitled, you can use "Post" as a replacement. For a Twitter post, include the text of the entire tweet in quotation marks, and use any capitalization and spelling used in the original tweet. Follow the text by including the date and time of the tweet.

> **Example 11a**: Try2BeLikeMe (Jay Kwellin). "Nothing Makes You Feel Better than Bacon." *Facebook*, 19 Dec. 2020, www.facebook.com/Try2Be224/posts/gheraf325667.
>
> **Example 11b**: Power to the Potato. "French Fries: It's what cookin'." *Instagram*, 6 Oct. 2021, www.instagram.com/tr35r5207t36100.html
>
> **Example 11c**: The Big Little GoldenSilver. "If you were here, YOU wouldn't be jealousssss." *Twitter*, 23 Nov. 2021, 12:44 p.m, www.twitter/com/BigLittleGS1/status/4546784378322.

Source	Citation
Book by a single author	Author's family name, first name. *Title of the book*. Publication details.
A book with more than one author	(e.g., Bracken, Daniel, Irene Parker, and Shawn Tully) *Title of the book*. Publication details.
Two or more books by the same author	1st book: Author. *Title of the book*. Publication details. 2nd book: ---. *Title of the book*. Publication details.
An article from a reference book	Author. "Title of section". *Title of the book*. Publication details.
A book with no author	*Title*. Publication details.
Government publications	Author. Government that issued it. Agency or department. *Title*. Publication details.
A translated book	Author. Title. Translated by. Publication details.
An article in a journal	Author. "Title of the article." *Title of the journal*. Publication details. Medium of Publication. Publication details will include the journal title, the volume number, and the year of publication (in parenthesis), a colon, the inclusive page numbers, and a period.
An article in a newspaper	Author. "Title." *Title of the newspaper*. Publication details. If the newspaper is in sections (A, B, C) then include the section and pagination.
An article in a magazine	Author. "Title." *Title of the magazine*. Publication details. Include the complete date after the title of the magazine followed a colon (:) and pagination.

💡 Tip

Citing Sources in a Non-English Language

In academic English writing, all non-English sources should be transliterated and translated into English. When using information from Korean language sources, all details including author, title, and publishing details should be written in English.

However, in order to aid research, it is best to also include the original non-English title with a translation in square brackets [ ].

Example 1: 김태훈 – 사랑의 힘 – 만화 출판사 – 2020
Example 2: Kim, Tae Hoon. *사랑의 힘* [*The Power of Love*]. Manhwa Press, 2020.

Activity 2

Use the following information to create a Works Cited page in your notebook.

Book 1

Authors: Don Brown

Title: The Thinking Man's Guide to a Better Birth

Publisher: Oxford University Press

Date: 2000

Pages: 109-110

Book 2

Authors: Ray Grant and 박화경

Title: Vampire Wars

Publisher: Hartman Murray

Date: 2007

Pages: 225-228

Book 3

Authors: William B. Irvine

Title: A Guide to the Good Life: The Ancient Art of Stoic Joy

Publisher: Oxford University Press

Date: 2008

Page: 26

Book 4

Authors: 이동식 & 김수빈

Title: 지진공학

Publisher: 한국지진공학회

Date: 2022

Page: 174

Government Pamphlet

Title: Find Your Seoul Date: 2021

Publisher: Department of Tourism and Leisure Planning

Government Agency: Ministry of Culture, Sports, and Tourism

Page: 21-27

Journal Article

Authors: Erik Collins & Kate Figueroa

Journal Title: Journal of Language and Culture in Modern Society

Article Title: Changes in Romanization of Korean Characters

Volume 106, pages 211-245

2008

Social Media Post

Author: Dain Moses

Title: My time at the 2020 Summer Olympics

Website: Facebook

http://www.facebook.com/dm7332/sfetg467

Comments Section

Author: YesWay2332

Title of video: Our Time is Now!

Author of video: SKKU4Life2000

Website: YouTube

Date of upload: March 2, 2021

http://www.youtube.com/#/skku1398abcd

After learning about what plagiarism is and how to avoid it, fill out both contracts. Remove the bottom contract, and give it to your professor. Keep the top contract for yourself to remind you about your commitment to academic integrity.

Plagiarism Contract

I, _____, hereby promise to uphold my credibility by avoiding plagiarism in my presentation materials. I will cite all the sources that I use from the Internet and from other places that are not from my ideas and creation. If I am caught plagiarizing or using materials from outside resources without proper citations, I will accept the consequences of receiving a zero on the project at hand.

Date: _____ Class: _____

Printed Name: _____

Student Number: _____

Signature: _____

_____

Plagiarism Contract

I, _____, hereby promise to uphold my credibility by avoiding plagiarism in my presentation materials. I will cite all the sources that I use from the Internet and from other places that are not from my ideas and creation. If I am caught plagiarizing or using materials from outside resources without proper citations, I will accept the consequences of receiving a zero on the project at hand.

Date: _____ Class: _____

Printed Name: _____

Student Number: _____

Signature: _____

_____

The Write Way

A foundation in academic writing for the humanities, business, and social sciences

Publisher | Ji-Beom Yoo
Printed by | Sungkyunkwan University Press
Publication date | February 19 2024

Writers | Bridget McGregor
       Cameron Bramall
       David Roberts
       Erik Figueroa
       Katrina Nicol
       Patrick Rousseau
Project Coordinator | Yoon, Yousook

Sungkyunkwan University Press
25-2 Sungkyunkwan-ro, Jongno-gu
Seoul 03063, Korea
Tel: 82-2-760-1253~4, Fax: 82-2-762-7452
http://press.skku.edu

ISBN 979-11-5550-401-7 13740